11 STEPS TO GETTING WHAT YOU WANT

11 STEPS TO GETTING WHAT YOU WANT

Persuasion and Influence in the 21st Century

Charles U. Larson

ROWMAN & LITTLEFIELD
Lanham • Boulder • New York • London

Published by Rowman & Littlefield
An imprint of The Rowman & Littlefield Publishing Group, Inc.
4501 Forbes Boulevard, Suite 200, Lanham, Maryland 20706
www.rowman.com

6 Tinworth Street, London SE11 5AL, United Kingdom

British Library Cataloguing in Publication Information Available

Library of Congress Cataloging-in-Publication Data

Names: Larson, Charles U.
Title: 11 steps to getting what you want : Persuasion and influence in the 21st century /
    Charles U. Larson
Description: Lanham : Rowman & Littlefield [2018] /Includes bibliographical references
    and index.
Identifiers: LCCN 2018041036 (print) / LCCN 2018041984 (ebook) / ISBN
    9781538118146 (electronic) / ISBN9781538118139 (cloth : alk. paper)
Subjects: LCSH: Persuasion (Psychology) / Influence (Psychology) / Success.
Classification: LCC BF637.P4 (ebook) / LCC BF637.P4 L357 2018 (print) / DDC 153.8/
    52--dc23
LC record available at https://lccn.loc.gov/2018041036

∞ ™ The paper used in this publication meets the minimum require-
ments of American National Standard for Information Sciences Perma-
nence of Paper for Printed Library Materials, ANSI/NISO Z39.48-1992.

Printed in the United States of America

To Mary, without whom . . .

CONTENTS

INTRODUCTION

Perhaps you chose *Eleven Steps to Getting What You Want: Persuasion and Influence in the 21st Century* because of its implied assertion to be able to help you get what you want. If so, you've made an excellent choice because it is targeted at persons who are interested in reaching their objectives in an orderly manner by using some of the proven techniques and/or tactics of successful persuasion and influence. Among those techniques is the making of a good first impression on prospects and/or other audiences and conducting in-depth audience analysis using a variety of research approaches which are discussed in detail in the book. Also included is an examination of the principle of reciprocity and the means to establish it with others by relying in part on high credibility, social proof, reasoning, evidence, and other forms of proof as well as one's own credibility, the building of which is also discussed.

A brief review of how to keep groups of prospects on track and moving toward one's objective is also included together with an in-depth consideration of the motivations of people who are faced with attractive proposals and persuasive offers. Since most persuasion occurs over time and is not the result of a single message or effort, I've included a discussion of campaigns for product types, brands, candidates, and worthy causes, to name a few.

Finally, I give several important ways to move one's prospect and/or audience to action and the ethics of persuasion and influence followed by ideas for marketing one's skills of persuading and influencing others. Each chapter includes a listing of "take aways" that one should be able to accomplish after reading that chapter by using some of the proven techniques or tactics of successful persuasion and influence. These techniques include making good first impressions on prospects and other audiences. They also include researching those prospects and/or audiences, and using reasoning and evidence to persuade them to accept one's proposals and/or offers by using high sources that have great social credibility.

I

ESTABLISHING ONE'S PERSUASIVE OBJECTIVES, STRATEGIES, AND TACTICS

INTRODUCTION

Each of us wants to be successful at persuading and influencing others—individuals and/or groups—in order to get what we want. A good way to think of it is that each of the twelve chapters in this book is devoted to a separate **Strategy** to be used to achieve that successful outcome. In order to help you prepare to use these strategies, I also include sample/example "scripts" as models for you as you prepare to persuade and influence. Sometimes they might be entire conversations, as is the case in chapter 2 where a salesperson is trying to persuade a prospect to use a new form of advertising. In other cases, these scripts may be only a paragraph, a sentence, or even just a phrase that will move the persuasive process to a successful outcome. Use these models as starting points for your own persuasive challenges whether they are at work, in your community, in your family, in organizations to which you belong, with a supervisor, or elsewhere.

The purpose of this initial chapter of *Eleven Steps to Getting What You Want: Persuasion and Influence in the 21st Century* is to give you an initial plan to get organized for persuading and influencing others—individuals and/or groups. As the title of this chapter suggests, three steps are critical. They are (1) Establishing an **Objective**. (2) Devising or identifying a **Strategy** or **Strategies** that has/have proven to succeed in persuading/influencing others. (3) Implementing the strategy/strategies by using specific and proven **Tactics** that have also proven successful in the past.

I have outlined and explained this three-step procedure using four brief examples—a military example; a retail business example; an organizational example; and a political example. In most chapters throughout this book, I have tried to provide typical "scripts" or example dialogues that you can use as models for your own persuasive and influential challenges. As noted above, sometimes they are extended presentations between a persuader and the target receiver(s). In other instances, they may be just a few or even one sentence. And sometimes, the example script could just be a short phrase. Whatever the case, feel free to adapt these "scripts" to best fit your own persuasion and/or influential situation and needs (e.g., a sales call, an attempt to recruit a volunteer, an attempt to prompt a donation, etc.).

Persuasion is a crucial part of every person's life, but few of us have studied persuasion in depth, and yet it impacts our economic, family, interpersonal, professional, political, and even our social and community lives. It is almost always preceded by having a degree of influence over those we hope to persuade. The overall goal here is to explain and demonstrate eleven ways (or tactics) to gain such influence, and as a result to successfully persuade others to change their behavior in some way. Perhaps you aim to change their purchase behavior, like buying a different brand of a product, or maybe you want to change their voting behavior or their level of donating to a worthy cause. Whatever your objective, you will have to employ some level of influence over these other persons, and then you'll need to use that influence to get them to follow your persuasive advice.

A MILITARY EXAMPLE

In military battles, there must be an overall Objective or a general goal like "Reduce or defeat the enemy's air, armored, and fuel resources." Second, there is/are a Strategy or Strategies for accomplishing that/those Objective(s). Strategies are usually something more specific and usually state a general action that needs to be taken, such as "Cut off their sources of supply" or "Destroy their means of communication." Finally, a Tactic or Tactics, which is/are usually much more specific like "air strikes on airfields, fuel supplies, runways, and the destruction of roads, bridges, and other bottlenecks by drones."

A RETAIL BUSINESS EXAMPLE

Successful and influential persuasion in business uses the same three elements. Consider a more typical economic example—a retail shoe store that has two Objectives in mind—reducing inventory and increasing its overall revenue. It uses the dual Strategies of advertising on local television during the 10 p.m. news featuring a local celebrity in the ads who offers the opportunity of a coupon for 20 percent off. Its Tactics include buying TV time on the 10 p.m. news and having a familiar and local news celebrity who will advise audience members to find the coupon in the sports section of the local paper.

AN ORGANIZATIONAL EXAMPLE

In an organizational example, a school board has an Objective of passing a bond issue in the next election. Without the added revenue, it will have to reduce its teaching staff, meaning increased class size at a time when classes are already crowded. It decides to use a Strategy of threatening to cut off all extracurricular programs in music, art, and athletics. This is a familiar strategy. The school board must be careful in the specific actions it takes. It decides to cut the programs on a trial basis just prior to summer vacation. This Tactic is specific and effective since it is only on a trial basis and only threatens track, baseball, and the arts programs of the choir and orchestra spring concerts. Also, its effects are experienced prior to the November vote on the bond issue.

A POLITICAL EXAMPLE

Candidates for a local political office use the same three steps. The candidate has the Objective of getting elected to office. One candidate has to use several Strategies. The candidate's first Strategy is to get yard signs and issue pamphlets printed with the candidate's name emphasized, and these can be seen by and distributed to potential voters. A second Strategy is to get invited to speak before various groups of potential voters. A third Strategy is to get the issue pamphlets made available to as many voters as possible. The candidate plans to use the following Tactics to implement the three strategies: The candidate's first Tactic is to use newspaper public service announcements and small ads to offer to speak before any group. The candidate's second Tactic is to distribute issue pamphlets to all attendees and to place a supply of the issue pamphlets in places where voters are likely to visit (e.g., the public library or libraries, city hall, the county courthouse, churches, etc.). The candidate's third Tactic is to have the yard signs placed at the homes of supporters by volunteers or by the candidate. So you see this pattern of Objectives supported by Strategies and implemented by Tactics applies in many contexts—even such contexts as persuading/influencing a travel club as to where or how to spend the next vacation. The individual interested in persuasion should do the same kind of planning. Begin with an Objective(s) and devise what you hope will be effective Strategy and use specific Tactics to reach your goal.

CONCLUSION

Before moving on to the major Strategies and accompanying verbal Tactics, I'll provide appropriate sample "scripts" for you to adapt for your particular persuasive situation(s) as mentioned earlier. Also you need to consider what verbal and non-verbal persuasive Tactics you should use in your persuasive encounters. Verbal persuasion refers to any communication that relies on words. Words are our most commonly shared and artistic means of persuasion. Now these words may be spoken, printed, broadcast, televised, whispered, printed on billboards or matchbooks, or sung in the lyrics to songs, to name but a few. This verbal persuasion could be offers made to prospective customers, voters, joiners, donors, supporters, believers, and others. They could also be statistics, evidence like witness testimony, and other kinds of verbal proof which will be considered in a later chapter. These could also include examples, stories, and dramatic narratives that make a point related to your Objectives or Strategies, and many more. Nonverbal persuasive appeals are any signals, codes, or symbols that do not rely on the use of words to convey persuasive or other meanings. They might be, for example, specific kinds of dress, like a nurse's uniform or camouflage outfits, or gestures such as pounding on the table with one's fists to communicate and emphasize critical points, as will your posture. The use of distance can also send messages, as when someone pushes into the "personal space" of others or refuses to sit next to someone. Facial expressions like smiles versus frowns communicate, as do eye contact and one's tone of voice. Many other movements all can convey meaning and should be considered when following the advice given here. So, as you approach a particular challenge calling for influential persuasion, don't take it too lightly. Instead, take the time to determine exactly what you hope to achieve. State your Objective(s) explicitly and clearly to yourself. Then do some research into what Strategies are available to achieve your Objectives using those given here as well as others you might find online or by looking at the websites cited and footnoted throughout the following chapters.

Then finally you should carefully rehearse your influential persuasion presentation. This is better done with a test audience—a friend, family member, fellow neighbor, or worker will suffice. It is the **UltimateTactic** in determining your success or failure. In using the advice given in *Eleven Steps to Getting What You Want: Persuasion and Influence in the 21st Century*, research that advice using internet resources. The following chapters each provide a major persuasive Strategy with verbal and non-verbal Tactics as well as easily adapted scripts for succeeding by using those Strategies and Tactics.

TAKEAWAYS

After reading this chapter you should be able to:

1. Discern the Objectives, Strategies, and Tactics in the persuasion and influence of retail businesses, organizations like school or county boards, and political candidates running for office.
2. Establish Objectives for getting what you want.
3. Determine persuasive and influential Strategies for reaching your Objectives.
4. Research and implement Tactics appropriate for the Strategies you have determined.

2

MAKING A LASTING, CREDIBLE, PERSUASIVE, AND ETHICAL FIRST IMPRESSION

You will recall from chapter 1 that we discussed the idea of using Strategies for achieving the overall Objectives, and our discussion noted that accomplishing these Strategies involves both verbal and non-verbal sample Tactics. I also promised you some sample "scripts" that could be adapted to a variety of persuasive situations (e.g., persuading family, boss, sales prospects, congregations, voters, coaches, and so forth).

What follows is an extended example of such first impressions involving an extended but hypothetical prospect for inserting a coupon in a cooperatively mailed envelope. Our prospect is Dr. Swenson, who is a local dentist. After discussing this example briefly, we will explore sample Strategies, Tactics, and scripts for achieving the Strategy of *Making a Lasting, Credible, Persuasive, and Ethical First Impression on Your Prospect(s)*.

Here's a script for a hypothetical dentist prospect (Dr. Swenson) that attempts to persuade him to advertise in a "Recent Mover" co-op mailing which puts his ad along with several others being sent to persons who have recently moved into his zip code. The Objective is to make a good impression on Dr. Swenson by the

Tactic of asking him a number of questions about *his* wants, *his* needs, *his* past successes and failures in advertising, *his* business, and so forth. The Tactic used research of a typical dentist's typical wants and needs by using online information that relate to dentists in general and using them in a script. Remember that wants and needs are not necessarily the same. The dentist may need new clients but really only wants families with children. I learned a number of things from doing both online and other research of dentists (such as exploring his/her advertisements, office premises, home address, etc.). The research showed that dentists want and need new clients to replace the clients that they lose due to their clients moving (20 percent of families move per year and do this every five years on average). The imaginary product—the Recent Mover co-op coupon envelope—provides Dr. Swenson with several benefits (e.g., ease of sending an attractive/enticing offer to new movers; eliminating the staff cost of designing, printing, and sending coupons; and discovering the mailing addresses of nearby new movers in the dentist's office zip code). Most persons who move to new zip codes want and need new professional service providers (e.g., auto repair, plumbing, handyman, doctor, etc.). Consider the Tactic and brief script to use it to design a script for your prospects.

VERBAL TACTICS

Verbal Tactic #1: Mention *them* by name and talk or ask about *them* and *their* interests, *their* activities, *their* business, *their* family, *their* history, and so on. It is pretty much common sense when meeting strangers to learn and repeat their names, and it underscores the impression that you are genuinely interested in them. It used to be called "making conversation." If you truly want to persuade them to behave, buy, join, vote, or to donate in a beneficial way, there is nothing insincere about such questions. In fact, they are genuine. What would a script for such a Tactic be like? Start out routinely. If your prospect is a small business person working in their store or office such as a local dentist, you might make an appointment for a twenty-minute meeting or even cold call. Either approach starts with something about their business location. For example, you could start with something like:

> *Script #1*: Ask about their business past and present.
> "Hi Dr. Swenson! My name is Charlie Larson, and I'm with Larson's Mailer, the coupon advertising company. This is the first time I have noticed your dental office. How long have you been in business here at this location? Where was your office before? Do you do family dentistry or some specialty like orthodontia? I see from the Little League trophies that you've displayed that you use sponsorship as part of your 'good will' marketing efforts. Do your kids participate in these sports? Do you or your spouse help coach or referee? What other kinds of marketing do you do?"
>
> Typically, dentists, doctors, physical therapists, and other professionals need new clients, so ask:
> "Do you lose clients through no fault of your own?" "Is that a concern of yours?" "Can you service more clients?" "How do you try to get them?" "How long do they stay?" This gets the prospect talking, and it gets you listening and learning—have a pen and paper or laptop handy to take notes. Get them talking about topics that interest them—basically themselves. Then start asking them about the details of their business.

Verbal Tactic #2: Tailor your presentation to fit your audience. Each audience you try to persuade will be different from the others in major or minor ways. As a result, it is necessary for you to change your language, non-verbal behaviors, and so on to fit that audience.

> *Script #1*: Ask about business specifics and tell them what you know—you've researched it.
> "Dr. Swenson, do you get many new customers in this neighborhood? The reason I ask is that I was just reading that the average person moves every five years. Can you believe it? That means 20 percent of our entire population is on the move

at any one time. I'm sure that many of those folks have moved away from their dentists and are looking for a new one. Why don't you consider putting a coupon with a strong offer like 'First and Second Appointments Free' or 'Free Whitening with Regular Appointment—Value $55!' in the Recent Mover envelope for your zip code. Have you ever tried an offer like that?" "I'll bet you'd get several new customers that way. What do you think?" "And the Recent Movers program reaches nearby homes for about $.40 per home. That's even cheaper than the cost of postage, and includes artwork, printing, addressing, postage, etc. You can add different variables like 'Homes with children,' 'Size of family,' or 'Family income.' Sending the coupon involves no labor for your staff. Otherwise, they'd have to do their own design and artwork for the coupon ad. Then there's the labor of inserting and addressing envelopes, and putting on a $.50 stamp, and mailing them. Could your staff do better things like re-activating dormant customers?" "Would you like to see some sample dentists' ads that have run in Recent Mover envelopes in other zip codes? I'll bring you sample envelopes with dentists' ads in them if you like."

Script #2: Point out how your offer can provide "payoffs" to your prospect.

"Dr. Swenson, you know that any investment you make is going to have a 'payoff' or a 'payout' for you." "Do you think that either option will be based on research you do?" "Do you conduct customer research yourself?" The Recent Mover envelope should work phenomenally for you. Just look at the past results."

Script #3: Show the competition's examples.

"Dr. Swenson, here are sample ads other dentists sent in one of our envelopes. Look at the payoffs to them. Do you think these offers would probably work for you too?" "These payoffs might come in increased business, customers returning for several years, and saving labor costs. Why don't you try the envelope on a two-time basis to test your return on investment?" "You can sign on for discounted mailings later once you've seen results. Then you can determine how much business you might get from a single family over five years—especially if they had two kids? And word of mouth might work with these new movers too. They might recommend you to their friends and neighbors as an extra pay off! I'll bet mailing an ad with an appealing offer to recent movers would have paybacks well worth the investment."

The key jobs here are to find out the prospects' wants and needs and to point out the benefits to them. Ben Franklin had a technique for identifying the pluses and minuses for many of the products and services he invented (e.g., the fire department, the lending library, lightening rod, and central heating). Franklin's method is both easy and effective and can be applied to the problem of influencing and persuading reluctant prospects.

You might have to do some online research on your prospect's business, political patterns, activities in organizations, and other things. When you feel fairly informed about their wants and needs, take a piece of paper and draw a line down the middle of it. On the left-hand side write down the unique attributes of your product or proposal. Beneath each attribute, list the payoffs it affords the user. I've done that for Dr. Swenson.

> *Script #4*: Demonstrate the product/service's attributes and resulting payoffs.
> "Dr. Swenson, the Recent Mover mailer has several attributes that yield real payoffs to you. Are you interested? O.K., here are some and the payoffs." *I've listed the attributes below with payoffs under them. You can build a script from them.*

- *Attribute*—Targeted consumer lists provided by Larson's Mailer. *Payoff*—Gets attractive offers to the most potentially profitable prospects.
- *Attribute*—Labor reduction in preparation and distribution of the ad. *Payoff*—Saves costs; boosts employee morale.
- *Attribute*—All steps in ad preparation are included for less than $.50/home. *Payoff*—Saves preparation, postage, list research, and labor by staff.

- *Attribute*—Professional ads get more attention and recall. Professional "look" to your ads. *Payoff*—Frees staff to remind clients of appointments, regular six-month exams, bills, contacting dormant accounts, etc. Saves time and money. Brings back "lost" customers.
- *Attribute*—Establish a relationship with a professional advertising agency. *Payoff*—A marketing staff to remind of next mailing. No research required.

Verbal Tactic #3: Summarize clearly and concisely as a signal that it's time for leave taking. Ask for them to list the three most important things they have learned from your meeting.

Verbal Tactic #4: Be sure to establish a way to "keep in contact."

> *Script #1*: "Well I've taken as much of your time that I intended, but together we discovered some key issues in the degree of success you can expect to experience in your __?__ (e.g., family, job, business organization, governing board, political campaign, etc.). If it's alright with you we could set a time—maybe early next week to meet, and I can fill in the details on how to approach your problems in your __?__ (family, job, business, organization, etc.). What about next Wednesday afternoon—say about 2 o'clock. I'll bring some more detailed maps, ads, and past successful offers.

Verbal Tactic #5: Be willing to admit your weaknesses as well as proclaiming your strengths. This reduces tension, and trust happens when we admit our weaknesses.

> *Script #1*: "Our Recent Mover envelope is, of course, just another piece of daily mail, but research shows that it gets sorted through. People go through it looking for pizza ads, oil changes, and handymen ads so they also see ads for services like yours."
>
> *Script #2*: "We're more expensive than other co-op mailers but our specially designed envelope has extra offers on the

envelope. Our cost is less than $.47/home—that's less than a first-class envelope, and price is the best indicator of quality and service in most cases. What about you?"

This script is just a model. Use it to build a script to fit your prospect.

NON-VERBAL TACTICS

What about the non-verbal things which help to make a good first impression? They are also very important in influencing and persuading others.

Non-Verbal Tactic #1: Show Up, On Time, or a Little Early or Call and Inform Them When You Hope to Arrive

Of course, the suggestion that you show up on time or even early is obvious, but many times the persuader doesn't show up at all. A large-farmland salesman in my home town didn't show up at all for a sales presentation when 600 acres were being sold. Think what that cost him ($12,000/acre x 600 x 6 percent commission). If discussion of your proposal develops, remember to have a pen and pad handy, and take notes along the way. The important thing is to communicate non-verbally that you are truly "into" the plan that is being proposed.

Non-Verbal Tactic #2: Establish and Maintain Meaningful Eye Contact

We all know that a dishonest used car salesman can't look you in the eye. If you're at a gathering and the person you're talking to looks over your shoulder as if looking for better pickings, you know that you're not important to them. You may as well cross that person off your list of prospects. Don't stare until the other person feels uncomfortable, so move your eye contact around the group, letting your gaze stay on one spot or person awhile and then redirect eye contact for several seconds before moving on to another spot, person, or place. Keep it direct but on the move, returning to your prospect(s) most of the time. If there is just one prospect involved, move your eye contact to their eyes, their chin, your notes, their eyes again, maintaining eye contact for 80 percent of the time you are speaking to the persons in the room.

Non-Verbal Tactic #3: Have a Well-Groomed Physical Appearance

Good grooming helps to make an influential, persuasive, and credible first impression. What follows is an in-depth elaboration on that factor in credibility. Just examine its many synonyms and enter one or more of them and the word "credibility" or "first impression" in any search engine and peruse the entries you find there. Here are a few of the synonyms for credibility: *authority, genuineness, validity, plausibility, trust, rigor, authenticity, integrity, recognition,* and *reliability.* Try to match your grooming and physical appearance to match your audience and the situation. You would probably dress differently for a meeting at a health club or a YMCA than for a meeting at a law office or a bank. Use mouthwash. Carry some breath mints too. Make sure your clothes are clean and pressed. Trim your nails and clean under them. Make sure your shoes are polished, tied, and appropriate for the situation. Make sure you have a good barber or hair stylist. You want to look professional, and good grooming is essential. Enhance the professional image you project by carrying a briefcase, a laptop, leave behinds, or even a manila folder with the prospect's name clearly imprinted on it. Another thing which helps make that good first impression involves the sense of touch. The largest organ on our body is our skin, and it's the most fundamental of our five senses. Touch in a first impression begins with the handshake, so practice being able to give a firm and confident handshake.[1] Researchers know that "there is a substantial relationship between the features that characterize a firm handshake—strength, vigor, duration, eye contact, and completeness of grip and a favorable first impression." So, yes, actually practice your handshake, with friends and relatives.[2] When shaking hands with an older person, be careful not to squeeze too tightly; they could have arthritis. Use secondary touch (i.e., the pat on the back or lightly holding the person's right forearm during a handshake, etc.). Touching is important, so use it with great sensitivity.[3] Studies also show that persons who keep their hands visible and gesture appear to be more credible than those who hide their hands in pockets, their laps, or at their sides. In fact, it is a good idea to keep all of our five senses—sight, sound, touch, smell, and taste—in mind when communicating non-verbally, especially in trying to create a persuasive, credible, friendly, and positive first impression. Think about how each of those five senses might potentially operate in your presentations to prospect(s). A friendly tap or pat on the back at the end of a presentation makes a good impression and signals that your presentation is done, and also that you'd like to be friends. There is also a kind of touch that directs a person to follow a certain path or direction. It is called a "control touch" and involves using one arm to point or gesture in the direction in which you want the person to move while the other arm should lightly touch behind the person's shoulder or lower back. Such an indication feels persuasive, warm, and friendly. By the way, avoid touching your own head since this signals boredom, and especially avoid touching your nose which is known as the "Pinocchio Touch." It is frequently considered by many people as a sure sign of lying.

Non-Verbal Tactic #4: Smiles Are the Best Kind of Facial Expression to Have When Trying to Make First Impressions

Smile! It is obvious that when trying to make a positive first impression on a prospect(s), that you can't go wrong with a smile.

However, you need to make sure your smile is genuine. It shouldn't be "glued on" throughout your presentation like the smile on a clown. Try to alter your facial expressions throughout your presentation.[4] Practice your smile in the mirror, and once you're pleased with the smile, lock what it feels like into your memory, and recall the expression on your face. And don't forget that most persons also smile with their eyes. Practice that in a mirror, covering your mouth and jaw with a piece of paper—like the NFL coaches do to defend against lip reading. Practice finding the right eye smile and lock that in too. It usually involves raising the eyebrows so that your forehead wrinkles at least a little.

Another trick is to remember to smile whenever you are feeling good,[5] even if alone driving the car or just reading or listening to music. Try to recall the feeling of a smile. Think of things, experiences, or persons that make you happy, and practice a smile. By the time you're done practicing, getting a genuine smile will come easier. And try to smile many times a day—make it a part of your waking life—it's actually healthy according to research. Also, it's easier to smile when you feel confident. I feel more confident when I have cash in my wallet, so when I go out to persuade, I make sure I am carrying at least $100 in cash in my wallet. Some persons feel more comfortable when carrying a certain "good luck charm" or when wearing a certain suit, shirt, and tie. And if you do get "wrinkles" around your mouth, eyes, and forehead when you practice a smile, you are "On Target!" Keep your teeth brushed and whitened to brighten your smiles. There are lots of products and treatments for that. You will become accustomed to having a smile on your face with practice. Use the same techniques for practicing other facial expressions like surprise, concern, or humor. The facial expressions soon come normally and are genuine. Three key words will help you achieve normality when you intentionally use your facial expressions to communicate. The key words are "Think," "Do," and "Remember" the feeling. *Think* about feelings of surprise or any other emotion; then *Do* or enact the facial expression that matches the feeling; and finally, try to *Remember* the feeling of that facial expression.

Posture and gestures are also signs of anger or confidence as well as other emotions like acceptance. An extremely useful catalog of gestures and body language can be found at: www. businessballs.com/body-language.htm#six-universal-facial-expressions.[6] Other facial expressions and gestures signal security, stress, emphasis, exasperation, "come here," boredom, "shhh," and more. Try to keep your arms unfolded (an "open" position) and show your palms instead of the back of your hands (indicates flexibility and willingness to compromise). Make a "bowl" gesture with your hands. It's a comforting and "welcoming" gesture versus an aggressive one. Cup your hands in the same way when rinsing your face. It sort of "says" that you have nothing to hide, and in ancient times it showed that you were not hiding a weapon.[7] (See the Allstate logo for a good model.) Other open non-verbal signals involve postures of confidence with feet fairly wide apart. If sitting, lean back but don't cross your legs. Spread out your materials on the table, desk, or countertop, and if standing, walk around a little.

Try to mirror your prospect's gestures (i.e., do what they do but in a subtle, non-mocking, way). Studies show that we unconsciously do this anyway to signal that we are friendly, trustworthy, and credible.[8]

OVERALL TACTICS

Overall Tactic #1: Make Your "Leave Taking" Match Your First Impression

Ending the persuasive presentation is critical. Research shows that the first, last, and most actions recommended in a persuasive presentation are the most memorable. Pay special attention to how you plan to end your proposal. Make our conclusion mesh with your *Lasting, Credible, Persuasive, and Ethical First Impression.*

Here are a few verbal tactics for closing. All of them can be used as a lecture-type closing format or in an interactive/audience participation format. Presenters tend to think that the audience perceives the presentation the way we do. Such misperceptions can lead to unpleasant, surprising results. Make your farewell a well-constructed and planned closing. Link it with one of the forms of summarizing discussed earlier. Though it might be awkward initially, it soon seems natural. Anytime you are persuading others, there comes a moment when you must "Ask for the Order" or the vote, agreement, commitment, or the action that is your overall Objective. It's called "The Close" in sales training, and you can do it in several ways:

The Get-Off-The-Fence Close

Faced with uncertainty, people develop fears and express them by stalling for time. It's O.K. to give them this, but only give them a short, definite time for a decision.[9] Usually, you'll hear one of a few familiar fears. Here are some fears and some scripts for defusing them:

Fear #1: "I don't want to spend so much in these economic times, and I need to be saving my resources."

> Script for Fear #1: "I hear that a lot. You have to know that your competition fears the same thing and hesitates spending on new equipment too. But remember, this is an investment not an expense, and it pays you back many times over and puts you ahead of the others. They're falling behind and will have a devil of a time trying to catch up with you. Good investments pay dividends almost instantly."

Fear #2: "I searched the internet for this equipment and others beat your prices. Why buy from you for more outlay?"

> Script for Fear #2: "They say that 'you get what you pay for' and it couldn't be more true for buying new equipment, and

that's because of service, not only quality. You see we're right here—not off in some corporate headquarters, and when you have problems, we're not 'next week' or minutes away nor 'when we get the parts.' My university decided to buy cheap personal computers for new faculty instead of Apple. You can guess where that led. They had to hire service experts to fix problems, and they're still on the payroll. Older faculty wanted computers too and insisted on Apple—not the cheap ones. They heard the horror tales from the new folks. And we have a lot of older faculty—many more than new ones. They insisted on the Apple brand. You can imagine it was a costly mistake. Then newer folks became jealous so that problems emerged later."

Fear #3: "I fear that some of my co-workers and others aren't going to agree with me on this decision. I'd like consensus on this. We have a steering committee. I'd like to go back to them and get consensus on this."

Script for Fear #3: "I understand, but no one bats one thousand. No true leader just ratifies unanimous decisions. Besides, there's always one grumbler on every committee. They simply disagree with everything. That's why you're leader—to make tough decisions—when there isn't consensus. If it were all up to the 100 percent agreements, any ninny could be leader. At some stage, you need to lead."

Fear #4: "One thing I really fear is built-in obsolescence. What if a new model comes out next year that's far superior to yours?"

Script for Fear #4: "This year was a major break through. There aren't any major innovations like that in sight soon. When they do arrive, I'll alert you and give you a fair trade-in on our state-of-the-art model."

Fear #5: "What if I make a bad choice? I'd get the blame. I could lose my job."

Script for Fear #5: "Well, one thing you have to keep in mind is that not to decide is a decision too. If you remember that, then making decisions is not so hard. If you've done your research, and you trust yourself—your character, your past decisions, and your values—you won't have regrets even if you are wrong this time. As Shakespeare put it, 'Our doubts are traitors, and make us lose the good we oft might win, by fearing to attempt.' To let doubt detain you from making a decision, even a wrong one, is poisonous to one's confidence."

Fear #6: "It's too hard. There are too many alternatives from which to choose."

Script for Fear #6: "Life equals alternatives. There are always too many alternatives. Look at the fast food alternatives at any major intersection or exit from a superhighway. People actually want choices. It makes them feel in charge. That's why they usually don't stop at the exit with only two brands of gas or fast food. *You* can't afford not to choose. The risk is too great. Steve Maraboli, author of *Life, the Truth and Being Free*, put it this way: "Make the choice to embrace this day. Do not let your today be stolen by the ghost of yesterday or the 'To-Do' list of tomorrow!""

CONCLUSION

By now, I think you are ready to begin to "achieve the strategy of *Making a Lasting, Credible, Persuasive, and Ethical First Impression on Your Prospect(s)*." In chapter 3, we will be discovering various ways to learn much about your prospect's demographics, socio-graphics, psychographics, needs, and wants. This makes that first impression easy, and you'll develop a loyal reciprocating base of customers, voters, workers, neighbors, etc. The research also helps you to widen your base via word-of-mouth recommendations in this age of persuasive social media. And true research keeps you from trying to manipulate.

TAKEAWAYS

After reading this chapter, you should be able to:

1. Establish Strategies and Tactics for making a positive first impression on your prospect/audience.
2. Identify your prospect/audience's needs and wants.
3. Ask relevant questions concerning ways to reach your prospect/audience's needs and wants.
4. Use the Tactic of referring to your prospect and/or audience by name.
5. Tailor your presentation to fit your prospect/audience's problems and situation.
6. Ask about specific business practices used by your prospect or audience.
7. Show the alternative offers made by the competition and discuss the strengths and weaknesses of those offers.
8. Demonstrate the attributes and payoffs of your product or offer.
9. Signal that your time/presentation is over.
10. Discuss the strengths and weaknesses of your product and/or offer.
11. Use the nonverbal Tactics discussed in this chapter, especially the use of eye contact and touch.
12. Have a well-groomed and appropriate appearance for the occasion.
13. End the meeting in an appropriate manner.
14. Answer any fears that your prospect/audience may have about your product or offer. Answer any questions about the details of your offer.

3

RESEARCH YOUR PROSPECT'S WANTS, NEEDS, JOB(S), ORGANIZATIONS, AND LIFESTYLE(S)

To influence and persuade others, you must conduct **Audience Analysis** on your prospect(s), and that means finding data/information about what they are like physically, socially, psychologically, and culturally. Remember that needs and wants are not the same thing. Dr. Swenson **needed** replacement clients, but he **wanted** clients with children. So, you should always find out what a prospect needs most (make that priority #1). Then find out what the prospect wants most (make that priority #2). Both objectives will require two kinds of research—*quantitative research* and *qualitative research*. Quantitative research measures amounts—things like income, height, weight, etc. Qualitative research measures the kinds and number of things in a category but not their dimensions or size; for example, the marital status of a prospect (married, single, divorced, or widowed). There is no dimension or size to a prospect's marital status, but it's useful to know if you're going to influence and persuade them.

Remember that earlier we talked about several different kinds of prospects one might want to persuade—potential customers, voters, fellow workers, members of the family, community groups, and so on. We could do quantitative research on our prospect(s) that would involve the dimensions of a certain variable (e.g., average income, range of income, age, or number of years employed by a company). We could also do qualitative research on things that have no dimension or size (e.g., their gender, religion, political preference, etc.). As a result, you can only evaluate the wants or needs anecdotally to use for influencing and persuading.

Chapter 3 explains and gives examples of quantitative things like a prospect's **Demographics** (e.g., income size, business expenses, or return on investment); and qualitative things like **Sociographics** (e.g., neighborhood type, lifestyle, affiliations, etc.); **Psychographics** (e.g., emotional response patterns, habits, social media uses and patterns, etc.); and **Ethnographics** (e.g., the communicative behavior in subcultures like speech patterns at a protest rally).

Psychographics differs from either Demographics, Sociographics or Ethnographics in that it tells you **WHY** clients/customers buy your product or service or why they vote for a certain candidate instead of how much/many of a given variable they possess, where they live, or how they communicate in a certain context subculture.

Researchers do Psychographics by asking the client, customer, voter, and/or typical prospects about their emotional responses to certain things such as varied lifestyles, their own lifestyle, habits, and behaviors. Ethnographics often studies the communication behaviors in a culture or subculture using case or "field" studies.

Let's look at what these four types of research reveal about a given set of prospects—business executives—a type of prospect you might try to influence and persuade to use your product or service or to donate to your worthy cause or politician's campaign. In terms of Demographics, the median (midpoint) pay for them is $50/hour or about $181,000 per year, and their educational level is a bachelor's degree. Only about 9 percent of them are women, and their average age is 57 years. Demographic data resembles the kind of information that the U.S. Census reports. One hundred percent of them say they use the telephone, email, and face-to-face communication every day. A graduate degree is usually required. About 60 percent hold either a bachelor's or master's degree.

In terms of Sociographics, top business executives usually live in exclusive suburbs, own and use new innovations like virtual reality, and affiliate with important community groups. They are also on Facebook and Twitter. Virtually all have and use a smartphone and desk or laptop computer. Many belong to the Association of Business Executives, and most belong to Kiwanis and/or Rotary. Sociographics tells you where they live, their lifestyle, and with whom they identify.

In terms of Psychographics, they tweet about things like McDonalds, Coke Zero, KFC, the Disney Channel, and BBC News. Nearly all of them said "playing golf with a business associate was a good way to establish a closer relationship." Nearly all play golf and are warned about golfers who cheat, and think that "the way a person plays golf is very similar to how he or she conducts business affairs." Close to one-third of them admit to moving to a better lie, and/or not counting tap-in putts. Why do they play golf? Well, 68 percent said they liked challenges and preferred a difficult course to an easier one. And 12 percent said that "golf is more important to me than sex" (www.nytimes.com/1993/07/13/business/company-study-executives-links-golf-business-similar-strokes-seen, http://abcnews.go.com/business, and www.onetonline.org/link/summary/11-1011.00).

In terms of Ethnographics, top business executives do things like negotiate contracts and agreements, appoint department heads and managers, identify places to cut costs and improve performance, and direct and oversee budget and financial activities. In small businesses, they may hire, train, supervise, and reward employees and are responsible for purchasing. In large businesses, they tend to develop and define policies, plan corporate strategies, and are skilled at deductive reasoning. They also need strong written and especially oral comprehension and expression skills.

What kinds of tools/methods do each type of data use to conduct their research? Demographics uses databases like the U.S.

Census Bureau, state driver's license and natural resources bu-
reaus, governmental, corporate, and private research databases
and/or reports. Psychographic uses varied systems for market seg-
mentation. One that has been used in the past was called the
V.A.L.s which stands for Values, Attitudes, and Lifestyles. To
quote from Wikipedia, "VALs . . . is a proprietary research metho-
dology used for psychographic market segmentation. Market seg-
mentation is designed to guide companies in tailoring their prod-
ucts and services in order to appeal to the people most likely to
purchase them." Users of the V.A.L.s system see consumers as
being included in one of eight categories of consumers.

For our purposes, top business executives fall into two catego-
ries, labeled Innovators and Achievers. Innovators have consider-
able disposable income and are willing to try new products and
technologies. As one source put it, "Innovators are successful, so-
phisticated, take-charge people with high self-esteem. They are
change leaders and are the most receptive to new ideas and tech-
nologies" and "Image is important to Innovators, not as evidence
of status or power but as an expression of their taste, independ-
ence, and personality."

Achievers are hard-working, goal oriented, family types, peer
oriented, private, and have a "me first" and/or "my family first"
orientation. They are in favor of the status quo and are politically
moderate (http://www.strategicbusinessinsights.com/vals/ustypes).

ETHNOGRAPHIC DATA ON TOP BUSINESS EXECUTIVES

As noted above, you can do Ethnographic research on your pros-
pects. Observe and record the everyday, ordinary behaviors of
your prospects. Let's suppose you wanted to know how promi-
nently to display a candidate's yard signs and bumper stickers.
Field research usually involves participating in the prospect's daily
activities so you might affiliate with a candidate for office. You'd
notice things like where the prospect's staff placed yard signs (on

the parking strip or in the yard) and bumper stickers (front or rear). By participating in the campaign you'd get some idea of how to approach your prospect(s).

CONCLUSION

This is not the whole story, and everyone doesn't do such sophisticated research. Furthermore, some influential persuaders either belong to companies or organizations that have staffs that do the above kinds of research or they can afford to pay professionals to conduct the research for them. And the future is bound to bring other and even more complex and sophisticated research methodologies. Nonetheless, the values of being aware of and of either doing this kind of research or having it done for you by the pros is clear. The more you know about your prospect(s), the better you will be able to influence and persuade them.

TAKEAWAYS

After reading this chapter, you should be able to:

1. Conduct an analysis of your target audience I terms of what they **need** vesus what they **want**.
2. Define and give examples of Demographic research that could be done on your target audience.
3. Define and give examples of Sociographic research that could be done on your target audience.
4. Define and give examples of Psychographic research that could be done on your target audience.
5. Define and give examples of Ethnographic research that could be done on your target audience.
6. Give examples and discuss how to target Innovators as a target audience for persuasion and influence.

7. Give examples and discuss how to target Achievers as a target audience for persuasion and influence.

.

4

CREATE A RECIPROCAL RELATIONSHIP BETWEEN YOU AND YOUR PROSPECT(S)

When I come up to the cashier at the supermarket, s/he usually asks, "Were you able to find everything you were looking for, sir?" And even if I haven't found everything on my list, I don't come back with "No! Your damned store doesn't have half the stuff on the average guy's 'must' list let alone everything I was looking for!" That sounds like a "crabby" answer. If that were a common way to communicate in supermarkets and similar contexts, the human community would be an unpleasant place in which to exist. No, in society after society, there is a "social contract" between most of its members to try being pleasant, courteous, and even helpful to one another. Maybe it is in our very DNA.

For certain, we are repeatedly taught it from childhood onward, as best-selling influence and persuasion expert Dr. Robert Cialdini, observed in his 2007 book, *Influence: The Psychology of Persuasion*. He calls it a *"Click . . . Whirr"* response, comparing it to the sound of the automatic "next picture" forward of a photo camera moving to a new frame of film. What he refers to is a subconscious and societal agreement that any human interchange usually begins with a friendly bit of conversation or a friendly action (like opening a door for another) that is usually followed by a reciprocal and also an almost obligatory, courteous, and friendly comment or action, such as "Thanks—I'll do it for you next time!" He calls this the *Principle of Reciprocity* and believes that it is a powerful tool of influence and persuasion.[1] Paleontologist Richard Leaky calls it "the very essence of what it means to be human."[2]

THE PRINCIPLE OF RECIPROCITY

Whatever the name you choose, when the Principle of Reciprocity is at work, a kind act or friendly word or action is responded to with an equal or approximate kind word or action. At least the great majority of the time, it is, and this is because we feel we sort of "owe" the other person for his or her kindness. It's as if we have an "obligation" to be friendly and kind in return. We are obliged to likewise be kind in word and deed. Cialdini says this Principle of Reciprocity is one of the main building blocks in his theory of persuasion.[3]

The Highway Patrol officer who stopped me recently for not following a traffic law surely believes in the Rule of Reciprocity. He had a kind word to greet me with through the side window when he asked for my driver's license, saying "Hi! I'll bet you don't know what I've stopped you for, do you?" instead of something a bit nasty like "Don't you know that you must pull into the left lane when passing an emergency or police vehicle with its lights flashing?"

By asking me this question in this way, he signaled to me that I was probably not aware of the practice of moving over to the left lane when approaching an emergency vehicle with its lights flashing—a practice that makes perfect sense but is not realized by that many drivers. It also signaled to me that he was offering me a little reciprocity and that I'd be smart to act humble. He too was trying to fit into that social contract, and so he said something courteous. In return, I reciprocated with something polite and apologetic like "Honestly, no I didn't know that. I know I wasn't speeding—the limit is 70 mph here, isn't it?" I tried to look ashamed, sorry, and really apologetic and said, "Could it just be a warning ticket, please, since I was unaware of that very reasonable regulation? I should have done that for safety purposes without even thinking. I was actually thinking about our visit to the Mayo Clinic in Rochester. We're on our way there now for my wife's surgery tomorrow." I think that he gave me that warning ticket because I was polite and apologetic in a reciprocal response to his question. I believe it was an example of the reciprocity principle in operation. Cialdini puts it this way, "The tendency among humans is that we want to give back to those who have given to us."

Ways to Create Reciprocity

Cialdini quotes from cultural anthropologists Lionel Tiger and Robin Fox's book, *The Imperial Animal* (1997), in which Tiger and Fox state that "we live in a 'web of indebtedness' and this web is central to the human experience, responsible for the division of labor, all forms of commerce, and how society is organized into interdependent units."[4] What a wise observation. How does one behave in a way that invites reciprocity? Cialdini gives us several helpful tips on how to create reciprocity. They are:

- **Be the initial giver.** For example, you should get the restaurant check the second it hits the table. You'll get it repaid somewhere along the line.
- **Don't give in hopes of getting something in return.** If you said, "You can get it next time," it might not be seen as a gift to them; quite possibly it's an unwanted trade and a burden.
- **Make sure the gift has benefits for the receiver.** "Gifts" should have real value to the recipient. Giving a stalled motorist a jump start with your jumper cables is clearly a benefit to the stalled motorist, and I'll bet that they would perhaps try to help any stalled motorist they came upon. It

probably wouldn't be the person who had helped them out, but it would be like reciprocally repaying the help they had received in the past. It's that "web of interdependence" that Tiger and Fox talked about. Maybe that's why free pens and calendars are so popular among both givers and receivers—they are useful and are usually kept. Furthermore, they have the giver's name and their phone number on them. They also can last a long time. I have kept a magnet calendar for 1984 because it has the Bear's Super Bowl season on it. It also has the phone number of the auto repair shop that handed out this "gift" to customers.

- **Offer information that is hard to find**. People appreciate information that is not easy to find. It's much more valuable if it's "inside" information and thus gives its receiver an advantage over the competition.
- **Give frequently.** One-time gifts are appreciated too, but if every year I get a calendar for the coming year from my State Farm agent right after Christmas, I feel I have been trained to always show up immediately after a client calls in an accident report and to drop everything else to help them. This also helps the relationship between the client and agent. It's interesting that State Farm trains and encourages its agents to offer other more meaningful and reciprocal gifts to their clients, of course, and to their community as well. They are urged to belong to civic interest groups like Kiwanis and Rotary, and they are to rush to community disaster scenes.

Examples of How to Use the Principle of Reciprocity

Let's take these tactics and create some hypothetical "scripts" that you can adapt to fit the particular persuasive situation that you face. Perhaps the department you work in has just held a welcome reception for the new department supervisor, and you happen to run into her in the company parking lot.

She says something like "Hi! I certainly enjoyed the depart-ment's welcome party last night." She's inviting you to reciprocate by using the friendly greeting of "Hi!" and her use of the word "party" and recognizing that you were at the reception. What if she had used the word "reception" instead of "party"? What are you going to respond with? A reciprocal response would be some-thing like "Yes, it was a fun time and so many showed up, and everyone seemed to have a good time visiting with one another and getting the chance to meet you on an informal basis." You've reciprocated her friendly invitation to interact.

Deciding "Who gets the check?" provides another typical chance to build reciprocity. There's always a guy who has to use the restroom when he sees the waitress moving toward your table with the bill. He's a cheapskate and always will be. If the group gets separate checks, he'll leave a tiny tip—maybe the minimum 10 percent, or maybe nothing. You'll never want to forge a real reciprocal relationship with him. You see that type always expects someone else to pay. Thank goodness there are those who'll snatch the check quicker than you'd believe. In fact, if you want to build reciprocity with the whole group at the table, just pick up the bill from time to time. You'd better be quicker than them or mention to the waitperson that you should get the check for the group when she first comes to the table. It puts "el cheapo" on the spot. So, your action serves as a double message of reciprocity. It per-suades the others that you are a good person to relate with, and so you've probably also made friends with some others at the table who are already familiar with "el cheapo" and his frequent rest-room needs, and you've probably influenced one or more of them to pick up the check next time.

Reciprocity and Persuasion

Reciprocity is not just a tool of influence. It is also a central tool and element of persuasion. If I do something nice for you (e.g., welcome you to the department, opened a door for you, given you valuable information, paid the bill, etc.), you are likely to feel obligated to reciprocate or to pay back. And there are several kinds and techniques of "Getting an I.O.U." like this. For example, a two-step form of reciprocation is achieved by asking for a lot and then retreating to a smaller and easier-to-accomplish act or word. Cialdini calls this one of a group of reciprocity-building tactics that demonstrates "reciprocal concessions." This persuasion technique is accomplished by reducing one's major request of the prospect by influencing them to feel an obligation to concede by agreeing with the second, smaller request. This happened to me not long ago when a volunteer for the American Cancer Society called me and assured me that they were not asking for a $100 donation, nor a $50, or even a $25 donation. They said they were only asking me to mail envelopes to four neighbors and sign my name. Those envelopes would, I guess, have requested money, but all I had to do was a little work plus the cost of first-class postal stamps. Like most everyone, I keep a pack of such stamps pinned up near where I write my bills so the request was an easy one. I said that I would send out the request cards. Soon after, I received the four envelopes, addresses, and request cards. The "reciprocal concession" I had made was to trade what I perceived of as a request for money for a small request of minimal behavior. I also made my own donation to the American Cancer Society.

Another tactic Cialdini uses to apply the reciprocity principle he terms "rejection-then-retreat,"[5] which also describes most union management negotiations, dealing for a new car or the purchase of a home, or the bargaining in the bazaars of the world. They all rely on the "Clicking and Whirring" of the reciprocal concession. They are almost always persuasive in the final result. The principle even works when the 2nd request is actually higher than the initial one in some cases, as the next actual case demonstrates.

Reciprocity and Free Offers

Research repeatedly demonstrates that people will buy, vote, join, donate, etc. more often when the requestor or persuader gives or offers them something for FREE! While neither you nor they are legally or morally bound to buy the brand that you've just tasted, you possibly feel or experience a sense of obligation to just do so. In another instance of the reciprocity principle in action, consider a similar occasion of the reciprocity principle at work in many "Worthy Cause" persuasive offers. I recently received mail from an organization called "Wounded War Veterans," and I have seen television ads sponsored by them also. They claim to help wounded military veterans to live somewhat normal lives if the recipient of the offer is willing to donate $19 per month. In the window of the envelope was a first-class U.S. postal stamp which was intended to be placed on the return envelope which would contain my donation of $100, $50, $25, or $19 per month. I would have felt awkward, even guilty, if I had simply kept the stamp and tossed the donation form letter and tossed the envelope in the trash, so I donated $10 and sent it off. Guess what? The next week I got another letter from Wounded War Veterans making the same appeal and again with the first-class postal stamp in the window, and that's the problem. Now I get the same letters quite regularly. Clearly, they have me on their list of "likely donors" who are worth another try.

The same type of example is the many worthy cause appeals that send you a "gift" of free return address labels with your name and address cleverly displayed. For example, Ducks Unlimited has pictures of retrievers on them. I feel a sense of appreciation for the stickers, and I know of the efforts of the Ducks Unlimited organization to preserve wetlands so I make at least a minor donation of $25. What is the lesson to be taken from these examples? When reciprocating, try not to make your feelings of obligation trap you. I read yesterday where only 60 percent of donations actually go to wounded veterans. They've already achieved more than a 900 percent return on their investment if you consider all those who do commit to having $19 per month automatically deducted from their checking account or debited to their credit card.[6]

There is also a kind of reciprocity between nations and states. For example, take the states of Minnesota and Wisconsin. They have agreed to honor one another's university in-state tuition costs. In other words, if you are from Minnesota, you may attend any Wisconsin university and not have to pay out-of-state tuition rates. Instead, you will pay in-state rates, and it's vice versa if you are a resident of Wisconsin. There are several reciprocity agreements between other states as well.

Between nations there also is a kind of legal reciprocity operating when it comes to extraditing accused criminal suspects or terrorists. There also often is a kind of reciprocity between states for recognizing one's professional licenses for attorneys, doctors, teachers, dentists, and so on. There is a sort of "Golden Rule" of reciprocity that you shouldn't take something unless you give something in return. Also, most cultures train their members in that golden rule from childhood onward.[7]

How can an influential persuader like yourself use reciprocity? What are some *tactics* of reciprocation? Here are a few web page tips that include reciprocity-creating applications that can help you be more effective at persuading others using the reciprocity principle. They will help make your web pages more friendly and effective in the ways they help potential visitors.[8]

- *Make your web pages easy to navigate.* It's persuasive and friendly and makes it much more likely that visitors will interact with the web page by pressing buttons and thus will go deeper into the page, and as a result they will learn about your services.
- *Break up your copy with bulleted lists.* They're easy on the eye and give a sense of organization to your proposal, and they make things easier to remember and use later as talking points.

- *Don't send "Push Alerts"* to your mobile shoppers too often. It becomes rude after a while, can be unfriendly, and can really turn people off.

- *Always ask for permission to send your proposal* (often called "opt in" email). It's polite and also friendly. And once they give you permission to send them a proposal, they've already made a partial commitment to it and are engaging in self-persuasion to some degree. It's like clipping out a coupon. By doing so, one has intended to make the purchase on which a coupon can be redeemed.

- *Always offer something of probable value to your prospect* on your web page or in your emails to them. It's a nice way to start a friendship and perhaps a business or other relationship that will have payoffs in the future, especially if the two of you have congruent or a very similar business or objectives. Giving beneficial gifts can lead to profitable partnerships.

- *Don't destroy your credibility* by asking your prospects for their present location if you're offering travel or really many kinds of proposals. People are already starting to fear giving away too much information about themselves. They might think you were "phishing" for information that could make them vulnerable to fraud.

- *Don't make it difficult for prospects to access your message* before they have been informed of what it's about. This is a cyber-tactic known as "phishing" by internet users.

- *Do send a sample of what you're offering* before making the prospect opt-in. It respects the user's time and efforts. Nobody really wants to buy something they haven't seen, and if you're proud of the brand or type of service you are offering, it shouldn't bother you to send a sample of what you're selling or of the kind of services you can provide to your prospects.

- *Avoid being overly aggressive in lead generation* (and in fact in all digital messages), and make the message brief or it will get deleted quickly. Again, remember that people are fearful about giving too much information about themselves away.

- **Don't write an essay or a lecture**—be conversational and read it aloud to make your rewrite "sound" more like conversation rather than writing. And reading your copy aloud will help you find your errors or awkward words. The ear is a much better editor than the eye.
- **Talk about your prospect/audience instead of yourself.** Ask them questions about their life, interests, family, and values. As noted earlier, people like to talk about things that relate to them and not what you are interested in or think. It makes it friendly and easy to read.

There are interesting words and graphics that capture a reader's interest and attention, and the bullets make it easier to remember what is said or written and to use the bulleted items as talking points later.

- **Try to use stories or narratives that would attract your prospect or audience's attention.** Human beings are born storytellers and love to hear and/or read them as well as to tell or repeat stories. Stories or narratives are going to be remembered much longer than lists of facts. The stories that we take away from a speech or sermon are what we recall long after hearing or reading them initially.
- **To make your copy readable, pretend sending it at $10/ word.** Then take out your editing axe and chop away to save bucks. You'll actually find the editing process enjoyable after a while. Keep a scorecard on how much you've saved by editing.
- **Ask the reader a question that they will respond to with a "Yes!"** It will precondition them to saying "yes" to the next question you ask. If you are lucky they'll say "Yes" to your offer, and besides, it's always more fun to say "Yes!" rather than "No!" isn't it?[9]

- *Be sure to analyze your use of social media.* Use one of the many analytical programs out there such as Google Analytics and some of their subprograms like Tag Management and Remarketing. They can capture some of those dormant accounts.

CONCLUSION

Well, after reviewing more than twenty ways to develop a reciprocal relationship with your audience members and looking at ways in which to say what you want to say by adapting the various scripts to your own situation, I think you are a little more eager to engage in influencing others in lasting, credible, persuasive, and ethical ways. This is especially true if you have gotten your target audience to "own" at least part of your proposal by researching their wants, needs, jobs, organizations, and knowing that those things create a *Reciprocal Relationship* with them. The topic we will explore in chapter 5 is the nature of proof which can really help you to influence and persuade.

TAKEAWAYS

After reading this chapter, you should be able to:

1. Understand and apply the "Principle of Reciprocity" in your persuading and influencing of others.
2. Understand and apply the five principles of gift giving to establish and/or further a relationship with others that is reciprocal and hence is both persuasive and influential.
3. Understand and enact the concept of "reciprocal concessions" as you try to persuade and influence others.
4. Understand and apply the advice given here on building a web page that will be helpful and effective to navigate.

5

PERSUADE OTHERS AND MAKE YOUR PROSPECTS *WANT* TO BELIEVE IN YOUR PROPOSAL

Given the **Objective** stated above for chapter 5 and following the layout of the several models discussed back in chapter 1, the next step is to state a **Strategy** and then to discuss various **Tactics** and provide accompanying scripts that will lead to success. For example, Overall Strategy—Give Your Prospects Evidence (e.g., Statistics, Examples, Narratives, Comparisons, etc.) Accompanied by Reasoning to Persuade and Influence Them.

The practice of persuasion was first codified by the Greeks and later the Romans. Both maintained that a person's beliefs (and related actions) come about through a combination of factors that include the persuader's reputation as well as their delivery, and most importantly, the evidence that is logically related to the behaviors and/or actions requested by the persuader via the rational reasoning process and emotional appeals or proposals. These codifications by them have been scientifically verified over and over again by modern-day social scientific researchers and under a variety of conditions (e.g., sales, politics, local government, counseling, coaching, preaching, interpersonal and public communication situations, and many more).

Let's briefly explore what these scientifically verified theories about persuading others have to say about using Aristotle's three types of influence. Then we can look at more modern interpretations, many of which grow out of the works of two of the most famous Greek and Roman persuasion theorists—Aristotle and Cicero.

Aristotle maintained that there were means of communication that served to persuade the Greek populace and the Greek Senate in matters of government, marketplace transactions, issues of the day, and various public presentations, to mention only a few. The three communication channels are:

1. One's persona, image, reputation, magnetism, or "charisma" (from the Greek χάρισμα *khárisma*). He called this type of evidence *Ethos*.
2. Logically related evidence (could include statistics, narratives, examples, comparisons, testimony, and other types of "proof" that can influence/persuade others), especially as it was processed using reasoning or types of logical conclusion drawing such as cause and effect. He called this *Logos*.
3. Emotionally prompted "evidence" which need not be logically related to the proposition (e.g., fear of crashing when using air travel or fear of having autistic children if administering vaccinations against childhood diseases). He called such proof *Pathos*.

The Roman rhetorical theorist Cicero later codified the five necessary steps/stages (or *Canons* as they were called) that were neccessary to be completed for persuasion to be successful. Though they probably date too long before him, they are:

1. **Invention** or the discovery (usually via research) of the available means of persuasion.
2. **Arrangement** or the selection and organization of the persuasive arguments and accompanying evidence.

3. **Style** or the coherent and more importantly eloquent and "artistic" presentation of the argument(s) or proofs (be it Ethos, Logos, or Pathos).

4. **Memory** or the rehearsal needed to present the persuasion extemporaneously. This Canon is commonly called the "lost" Canon since persuaders rarely memorize presentations today. Nonetheless, it's best to at least memorize an extemporaneous version of your presentation.

5. **Delivery** or the effective use of posture, eye contact, gestures, voice, metaphors, and other techniques in the actual presentation of the persuasive proposal (e.g., PowerPoint).

Later students have been looking for and discovering further clues to the secret of successful persuasion examining variables like appearance, dress, gestures, vocal quality, height, attractiveness, and charisma. For our purposes, in chapter 5, we will examine a variety of kinds of evidence and reasoning having the most persuasiveness in the situations and audiences most of us encounter daily. We will include "scripts" for introducing and explaining these proofs to our audience(s) or prospects, and you can feel free to adapt them in any ethical way.

In any given persuasion situation, do not try to manipulate the audience via trickery, hyperbole, falsification of evidence, faulty reasoning, etc. For example, a frequently misused and potentially manipulative kind of evidence used to prove something to an audience or a prospect is the use of misleading statistics. But there are ways of using ethical and non-manipulative statistics that really do persuade. There also are ways of using statistics that work but which are manipulative/unethical. There are yet others which are manipulative but may "boomerang" and lead the audience to a completely opposite conclusion than the one intended.

Think of ground beef as 75 percent lean versus advertising it as being 25 percent fat. Both are ethical and non-manipulative. Which use of the identically same statistic would sell more packages of the product? Statistics can mislead due to the sample size they represent and when, where, and how the statistics were counted. Say a dozen out of 100 drivers said they always pull over and park when using a cell phone. Does that mean 12 percent of all drivers in the nation do this? What if the sample of 100 were semi-truck drivers interviewed by a person speaking with a foreign accent versus being interviewed by a female Caucasian highway patrol officer at a truck stop at 3:00 a.m. during a blizzard? The statistic would be far different if the sample of 100 were sixteen-year-old males preparing to take their driver's license test, I'll bet.

Or consider a brand of "low calorie" salad dressing that advertises that it has 40 percent fewer calories." The wise consumer should ask "40 percent fewer than what—maple syrup?" How about this one? "Half of Americans do not know that Judaism is older than Christianity." Or take sales figures for retail stores. A department store runs a "Ground Hog Day" sale early in February 2014, as well as its later "Hatchet Day" sale on President's Day. They tallied up the sales figures. Surprisingly, both sales are far lower than last year's tally for President's Day. The Ground Hog Day sale idea was new. Is that why it tallied best? What should they conclude? From past statistics, February sales all tend to do poorly. Maybe it's the weather? Is that it? Statistics show that nearly all discretionary dollars are spent on the two biggest spending holidays—Christmas and Halloween—fewer are available to most consumers in February. As a result, it's not wise to spend much in the 1st quarter. I suppose that's why so many sales (e.g., Valentine's Day, President's Day, etc.) are in the first quarter. They reduce inventory, and retailers hope to induce consumers to spend on things like home improvements (e.g., remodeling the basement), clothing, and appliances.

Has the retail department store drawn a faulty conclusion? Well, there isn't a true cause/effect situation here. You see, February 2014 was about the coldest, snowiest, and rainiest February on record. This mistake in drawing a conclusion is called "a fallacy of defective induction" or a "hasty generalization" which is "studying a single case, and generalizing that to be representative" (www. wikipedia.org/wiki/Faulty_generalization and www.abcnews.go. com/GMA/video/cost-polar-vortex-21458433).

Sometimes the faulty conclusion is the result of what is called an "intervening cause," as in this case, if you're using evidence to influence and persuade be sure you aren't drawing a hasty conclusion by relying on poor samples or forgetting intervening causes. Aristotle held that an emotional argument (like a Fear Appeal) could trigger unpredicted responses like anger and hostility to the messenger versus the actual cause of the fear. Fear and anger are opposite sides of the same coin. Both are also used frequently in popular advertising (particularly in political ads) telling of dire outcomes if a certain product isn't used, if a candidate is elected, or if a policy is legislated (e.g., gay marriage, legalization of marijuana, right to die, etc.). The other side of the coin is that great things will occur if another candidate wins or a certain policy is enacted (e.g., a new tax).

A Fear/Anger Appeal is used in a television ad in which a healthy and vigorous elderly person falls in her kitchen and cries out "Help! I've fallen down, and I can't get up!" The announcer then says, "You can get a Life Alarm device for free! And you'll never be afraid of being alone again." Fear Appeals are also the "stuff" of many health related, retirement funding, and identity theft ads also. A tough one is when the highly emotional and fearful term *global warming* is mentioned. Many simply reject it and tune out just as they did when the very early smoking and cancer alerts came out. Suggested alternate language for global warming, which is more comfortable, might be *climate change, pollution, health*, or *extreme weather*.

Choose words that are the friendliest and that don't cause fear/anger. One problem with Anger/Fear Appeals is that they sometimes can also have a result beyond a refusal to believe and intentional forgetting (sometimes referred to as "selective retention"). Instead, they result in an outcome that is the reverse of what was intended. Recent researchers call this the *boomerang effect*, and you can understand why. The result may be the exact opposite than that which was intended.

For instance, the prohibition of sales and serving (but not the consumption) of alcohol in the 1920s was intended to reduce crime, spousal and child abuse, alcoholism, shiftlessness, being late for work, hangover effects, and more, but it actually resulted in less respect for the law, corruption of police, politicians, and judges. And it ignited and ultimately led to organized crime, increased cigarette smoking, eliminated regulation of "pure" or safe alcohol leading to impure bathtub gin, reduction of government revenue, gambling, prostitution, and had many other negative effects. So before using emotional appeals to fears, consider the possible unintended consequences that might occur (www. wikipedia.org/wiki/Unintended_consequences and www.patheos .cd its spacing and alignment om/blogs/unreasonablefaith/2009/03/ 12-bad-effects-of-prohibition-you-should-know).

And there are other appeals using Pathos, that must be carefully used or they can lead people to lose control and act irrationally (e.g., marches or demonstrations that lead to mob violence or civil chaos). Nonetheless, anger and confidence are powerful emotional motivators, or as Jeremy Porter notes, "In a two horse race, emotion, not reason, wins the race." The Anger/Fear Appeal rarely wins the day.

If you've dealt with an angry neighbor, an angry parent, or an angry customer of the product or service you represent, you'll be familiar with the ineffectiveness of an angry persuader. They are usually communicating anxiety or fear, "and therefore, at some level, a weakness." And fear or anger are usually contagious and can lead to nasty interchanges. They are rarely effective in bringing about change, are remembered, and may result in people holding grudges or wanting revenge. Persuaders ought to try to avoid a situation that makes you or your prospect(s) angry or fearful. It certainly does not help you to make friends and is very rarely effective in influencing or persuading others. Fear/Anger are incompatible with confidence, leadership, and charisma. Anger subtly tells others that you are really just afraid or maybe dangerous. Anger doesn't expedite or emphasize persuasiveness. And trying to use anger to persuade never builds true charisma nor results in persuasive success. Aristotle also mentions the dynamics of the *pleasure/pain* principle.

Everyone wants to avoid pain. There are two sides to this coin also. We either try to seek pleasure (e.g., pride, appreciation, etc.) or to avoid pain (e.g., disapproval, shame, or embarrassment). Many television ads use these emotions. For example, the pleasure you'll get and the pain you'll avoid with the newest feature from Ford—a tailgate that opens your SUV or minivans's rear door with the touch of your toe. So, you see there are many advantages to using Aristotle's virtues and vices in your persuasion.

It is reassuring to know that his principles have been verified over and over again by countless scientifically conducted research studies. And giving the choice of pleasure versus pain can help your persuader financially and thus ease future sales without having to make decisions. If you're trying to convince them to move to a new job, consider the result of this study. Researchers asked workers to rank the top ten factors in their satisfaction with their jobs. Then they asked managers to rank the ten same factors in job satisfaction. Guess what? The factors ranked in the top three by workers were ranked eight, nine, and ten by their bosses who ranked "Pay" as #1, "Benefits" as #8, "Benefits" as #2, and "Work Conditions" as #1. What did the workers rank in the top three places? They said that "Appreciation for job done" as #1, "Fellow workers" as #2, and "My boss listens to me" as #3. What did the new company offer the workers in terms of their top factors? Very little.

Well, what would a good retail sales *Pathos* script be? Experiment with that challenge.

My script goes like this: "With the economy recovering slowly, you need to give your customers a 'sense of urgency' about getting their fashions for next fall and winter *EARLY!!!* Prices are at their lowest to clear the shelves, and there is still a good selection. You could advertise something like *'FREE Scarves with Any President's Day Sale Purchase!!! Good Only for a Limited Time While Supplies Last!!!'* Scarves are high profit/low cost aren't they? So put in a coupon for the free scarf in the *'Save Now at the February Beat the Competition Back to Next Fall' fashion issue of the MID-WEEK.'* And we're offering a 25 percent discount on column inches if you sign a year-long contract—that'll get customers in here and thinking they'll get the jump on the competition. And people will think of you first. That's sure better than being a Johnny-Come-Lately operation in July like most clothing stores do, and you'll reap the profits really early this year." Now there is no *NEED* to have one's daughters dressed fashionably when returning to school in the fall, but there sure is a *WANT* to have them dressed to keep up with the rest of the other returning daughters. The customer gets a major win as a great parent, and they'll be experiencing confidence and pleasure instead of pain. You are probably thinking of ways to persuade at least some of your audiences and prospects. With advance notice, remember to be careful with using the appeals and the words you use—they can either work for you, or they can "boomerang." They can trigger thoughts, beliefs, hopes, fantasies, and dreams for any audience or prospect. Enough of a warning; let's now proceed to the third channel of persuading others discussed by Aristotle. These persuasive strategies have also been verified by scientifically conducted studies.

This third channel was called *Logos* by Aristotle, and we get words like "logical," "logo," "illogical," "logistics," and "cogent" from its root. The word was even considered a synonym for the "Word of God" in some religions, as in "the divine wisdom manifest in the creation, government, and redemption of the world" and "reason that in ancient Greek philosophy is the controlling principle in the universe." So, you can see that it must be powerful in persuading others. What did Aristotle mean, "Logos is the appeal towards logical reason"? If the speaker wants to present an argument that appears to be sound to the audience, Aristotle stated that it "should prove something or at least it should appear to prove something." Another source tells us that "Logos is the Greek word for WORD (http://pathosethoslogos.com/).

A more common type of evidence which we use to persuade is often used to sell people on a certain idea, political candidate, or way of thinking. It goes back to our differentiation between NEEDS and WANTS. One example offers instances of this kind of evidence and how to use it. The persuader presents evidence showing that You Need It! referring to the idea, brand, idea, or the acceptance of a proposal. A script for this might be "You need to vote for regulation of handguns, given the everyday 'gang murders' in most large cities" or "You need some time off" or "You need a good night's sleep."

Another approach deals with one's worthiness in getting a product, reward, change, or proposal, as in *You Deserve It!* A script for this one might be "After all the effort you put out in accomplishing the project, you deserve a great bonus!" or "You deserve to treat yourself to this trip to Branson, Missouri as a reward for surpassing the sales quota." AT&T's ad features a young male grade school teacher asking a small group of his students if he should get a fast car or a slow car. Of course, they all reply "A fast car!" emphatically, and when he asks why, they reply "You deserve it!" repeatedly while dancing and gyrating for the rest of the ad. The Duluth Trading Company tells prospects they deserve better durability than regular clothing that tears, gets soaked, stretches, binds, etc. Another appeal dealing with the WANTS/NEEDS dyad is *You Should Just Try It!?* and the offer promises free trials or samples. That's why the auto salesperson wants you to take a test drive or why they give away free tastes in the supermarket.

The persuader may emphasize *The Sin of Guilt* in that unless you participate fully, the whole project might fail or we may miss the goal or lose the game. In other words, "We're Counting on You!"

Another appeal might be "This could be the only *One-Time Chance* for us to offer a La-Z-Boy recliner at this price." The strategy here is to emphasize the short supply that is available. Buy Now!   (http://www.lifescript.com/well-eing/articles/p/persuasion_techniques).

Quality versus Quantity is pretty well understood, as is its half-sibling *Quality versus Price*. It's a strong kind of evidence to demonstrate that the more expensive version of a brand, education, program, or policy is well worth the higher investment. The cheaper or "more bang for the buck" proposition can be overturned by citing evidence that the more expensive version simply outlasts, outperforms, and outsaves the competition. "We Cover the World" is the way Sherwin-Williams paint products shout out their market success.

The "Good Citizen" approach appeals to the audience's or the prospect's civic obligations. It relates to endorsements of brands, candidates, ideas, societies, or even the nation's well-being. These endorsements could be by individuals, societies, informal groups, brands, or organizations such as unions, political parties, government bureaus, and others. The Good Housekeeping Seal of Approval is an example as is the Underwriters' Laboratory Seal of Approval or endorsements of political candidates by the United Mine Workers of America or by newspapers or even by other office holders. Even the endorsements of famous athletes or celebrities can be considered this kind of persuasion. Basically, the appeal assumes that the endorsement is obvious evidence of approved housekeeping or electrical practices, or of certain candidates' beliefs and platforms or of certain brand qualities. A script using this kind of appeal might go something like this: "Well if the United Mine Workers think that accessible healthcare for everyone is a good idea, then so should the average working person" or "Remember that 'Buy American' is good for the U.S. economy when shopping for computers" or "Air Jordan athletic shoes are the best for really jumping high and far!"

Another appeal that can be repeated over and over again in advertisements, sales pitches, political speeches, and elsewhere is the Benefits versus Features pitch. I don't particularly care if a certain brand of automobile has "aerodynamic styling" (a feature), but I can really be persuaded if it gets good miles per gallon (a benefit) and looks sexy (another benefit for some). As in the case of buying a home versus renting, the thoughtful persuader gives a lot of time to consider the many benefits which can accrue to the brands, candidates, policies, and practices that s/he may be promoting, as opposed to what features they have. For instance, too often the salesperson tells us that a feature of buying your own home instead of renting is that with buying, you get "privacy" away from next door or down-the-hall neighbors. But they often forget to mention the tax deduction benefits, the benefit of building equity that could serve as a line of credit, the benefit of using the home as collateral for a loan, its benefit of projecting a certain image, its benefits for child-rearing practices including the benefit of privacy from other kids, and many more. A script for using this kind of evidence might come in the form of a question, such as "Don't you think getting the check from the IRS refund in May is a plus?" (www.lifescript.com/).

Let's go back to good old Dr. Swenson. I learned that the new mover *feature* of the envelope gave him new potential clients moving into his zip code. But I never realized that the odds were so high; that 20 percent of the population in any given zip were new movers. After I asked some questions about his WANT to capture the business of new movers, both he and I realized that the new mover feature also had additional benefits. The ad and its "Free Whitening" offer reminded former clients of what a congenial dentist he was and how good he was with kids, and that fact resulted in rejuvenating clients he hadn't seen in ten years or more. It also resulted in word-of-mouth advertising. And the "no-effort involved" in sending the envelope freed up staff time to promote his offer on teeth whitening by phone.

So you see, stressing the benefits of the presentation and related proposals to his audience(s) not only is persuasive but also gives good reasons for becoming friends. Now the above examples point out the differences and the connections between reasoning and evidence or proof.

British logician Stephen Toulmin points out three elements of a persuasive argument in his book, *The Uses of Argument*. He refers to the everyday persuasive appeal when he points out that the first element in any persuasive argument is the *Claim*. It is the thing you want your prospect(s) to accept, believe, and act upon. In his model, the Claim is the first step in everyday persuasion, so claim what you want to get or prove, plain and simple, no tricks, no manipulation, just a plain and simple Claim. For example, in the beauty shop instance, the script would be something like "I think I can increase the number of persons in your loyal clients list using the Recent Mover envelope, and it won't cost as much as your yellow pages ad, and you'll get a coupon attached that'll have your name, address, and telephone listing in it." If the prospect buys that proposition initially, you have already succeeded. However, if they question the claim, saying something like "I don't believe it!", Toulmin then recommends a second element called *Data* in order to convince the doubter. It is equivalent to irrefutable evidence. In the above case, price lists for the Recent Mover envelope and the local yellow pages directory should be enough to do the trick. It's always a good idea to have a yellow pages price sheet packed with you when making a persuasive advertising call. The yellow pages are usually the most expensive competitor in town.

Usually the Data (see below) does the trick, but occasionally there is a prospect who still has doubts and says something like "I still don't see that that proves your case. It doesn't convince me." One must then try to explain the reasoning process, the pedigree of the data, or show that there is no other possible explanation for your claim.

Toulmin offers a simpler and more marketplace model of persuasion. When you think about the everyday persuasion you use, you usually begin with a Claim. For example, you might say something like "Why don't we split the costs of planting a row of evergreens along the back property lines of each of our lots so we block the view of the Section 8 apartments?" You just make a Claim. Let's suppose he responds with "What's so bad about the apartments—each has its own parking place?" He's asking for Data. You might respond by saying, "Well, the bad thing is that the police say that there's lots of drug dealing going on in the parking lot, and that might lead to violence in our back yards." You've just given him the Data and the reason it supports your Claim.

Toulmin calls this explanation of your logic the *Warrant*. The drug dealing = Data (police verified). The connection with potential violence is the reasoning or the Warrant that the Data support the Claim. It's clear that Data serve as the fulcrum upon which entire arguments are decided. If the Claim isn't rejected, there is no need for Data. If the Claim is rejected, you must proceed to Data and determine if it suffices. If not, you must explain why it does prove the Claim by using some Warrant.

TYPES OF DATA OR EVIDENCE

We spend most of our time in this section discussing logical evidence, but there are a couple of other things that don't immediately come to mind. For example, Ethos is a kind of evidence too. High Ethos proves why one should follow the persuader's advice. It "says" that the persuader is a highly credible and consistent source. And we also examined Cicero's stage of persuasion called the *Oratorio* or the delivery to the audience. This included such things as posture, eye contact, vocal tone and volume, and physical gestures. These also served as a kind of proof or evidence about the persuader in everyday persuasion. However, there are Data or Evidence that proves the advisability of courses of action which you advise. We already saw one type of such evidence in the very effective use of statistics which persuade and are easy to locate using a search engine. The use of statistics demonstrates the "Before/After" approach to prove a Claim that the well-being of a society, a class of people, an organization, a company, a church, a school system is either better off or worse off after the introduction of something new.

Also, sometimes you can present statistics in a visual approach by using graphs for receivers that don't grasp the numbers alone—either bar graphs, pie chart graphs, or line graphs work well. Most of you are already familiar with this way of dramatizing statistical proof, and it's excellent to include it in any kind of "leave behind" materials you use in your persuasive presentations. The "leave behind" could be a price list, chart, brochure, or a business card—they're easy to remember, last, and will remain long after your presentation   (http://www.basic-mathematics.com/images/ linegraphs.gif and http://www.basicmathematics.com/images/).

As noted, *Examples* are another kind of evidence which you can use to convince your prospects using everyday persuasion. Really, they are one-time instances of many statistical proofs and are easy to remember and use. Start collecting them in a file today. Let's suppose you want to convince a prospect that they should institute a certain business practice—say doubling the customer's money back when not satisfied with their purchase. They read somewhere that it could lose them money. In actuality, very few persons ever take the retailer up on the promise, and yet it sounds good; Walmart is a good example. They offer to match prices of competitors or a "double your money back" guarantee on produce if the customer isn't satisfied—just bring the produce back and get a voucher for double the cost.

The Example is powerful evidence in this case, especially for anyone who has had to return an item—the lines are long and boring. Here's another case relating to the idea of promoting *Generosity*—something most churches want to persuade the congregation to practice. What if you see an old guy holding a sign that says "Homeless and Hungry. Please Give!" You open your wallet to find only a five, a ten, and two singles. Which will you give? I'll bet the two bucks. But what if just then right ahead of you, a young girl carrying a sack from Subway stops, opens the sack, unwraps the foot long, and gives it to the old guy along with a bag of chips. Now what does Generous mean to you? You have just seen a person give up her entire lunch which is probably worth close to $10 to the homeless guy. After that, you'd be much more likely to fork over the $10. She becomes an example to you, and the entire event could be retold at Pledge Sunday at church as an incentive.

Again, the internet can be a life saver by entering the word "examples" followed by a few words describing your persuasive objective. So, when searching for Data to convince your prospect, don't forget to look for relevant and persuasive Examples. Many can be drawn from your own experience and memory. Also, keep a file of them.

Dramatic Examples, Narratives, and Anecdotes are another kind of persuasive evidence which you can use to convince your prospects. Really, they are one-time instances of numerous statistical proofs and are easier to remember and use. Start collecting them in a file today. Here's one that proves that judgments are often very debatable:

Three umpires were discussing how they called balls and strikes. The first umpire says, "I calls 'em as I sees 'em!" The second umpire says, "I calls 'em as they are!" The third umpire wins the contests when he says, "They ain't nothin' until I calls 'em!"

Here's a hypothetical Example relating to the idea of promoting always driving less than the speed limit. It used to drive me nuts as a teenager to ride with Dad for five hours to a fishing spot at 55 mph or 10 mph less than the limit. Once I got my license, I tried to drive at least the limit or a few mph over the limit because my friends told me that the cops didn't mind people going as much as seven mph over the limit—they did it themselves. Then I got a ticket for speeding just two mph over the limit. You guessed it—my Dad said, "Well, I hope you learned your lesson—I've never got a speeding ticket in more than 30 years of driving!"

The Narrative or mainly true story is probably the most powerful form of persuasive evidence an everyday persuader can use. I, and many others, believe that a basic human impulse is storytelling. Think about it for a moment. One of the first things we ask of our mutual friend upon meeting a new stranger is "What's his/her story?" Most public speakers try to begin their presentations with a joke or a narrative. Or we hear of an unusual event like the transmission falling out of your neighbor's car. What do you say? "What's the story on that?"

Or consider that the parts of almost every sermon that are remembered an hour later are the stories or examples, and what is a Narrative but a single example. Statistics tell a story as well. Jesus taught most of his memorable lessons using parables which are a form of the story. A good story allows the speaker to raise emotions "naturally" and also presents the solution to the problem in an indirect manner in the form of the outcome.

What does it take to make or use a good story or Narrative? Well, there are several central parts to a Narrative or a good emotional and audience/prospect-involving story. A story is the kind of evidence that allows the speaker to raise emotions naturally and also to present a solution to the problem in an indirect manner. Stories are also memorable. One of the central elements is good motivated characters or Roles. It's sort of like there must be good and positive characters or Roles and equally bad, evil, or wrong characters or Roles in the story. "Little Red Riding Hood" would go nowhere if there wasn't a big bad wolf. She'd just bring some cookies to her sick grandma. Nothing interesting about that, is there? Then there must be a background, place, or *Scene* in which the good story takes place. Little Red would be pretty dull in a city, wouldn't it? Well, it could be revised for the city with Red being a fashion designer bringing some new designs to Gram's Fashion Firm and Wolfie being a competitor planning to steal the designs, thereby ruining Gram's firm. The Scene should be appropriate for the next element of the good story, the Act, action, or plot to occur. The movie *Psycho* couldn't very well take place in a Holiday Inn could it? It has to take place in the weird, scary, lonely, and deserted Bates motel where there's no free WiFi or continental breakfast or a pool and a sauna. In other words, the Scene must be an "appropriate" container for the action or acts that are about to be taken in their assigned Roles. In the Bates Motel, Marion should be trying to act normal even though she's just stolen $40,000. She doesn't even ask to see a sample room before registering for the room she's going to be murdered in (http://academic.research.microsoft.com/Publication/2576277/a-grammar-of-motives).

So before using a Narrative as Data or Evidence to prove a Claim to a prospect, think of it as telling a story that has characters with roles that are going to impel them to take action in a scene. There should probably be good characters or heroes and bad characters or villains. None of your stories or narratives will be as dramatic as *Psycho* in all likelihood. Probably the easiest and most likely persuasive use of narrative in a situation is one that grows out of the context. Say your prospect is a church's building committee and you're going to convince them of sending a single bright penny and a brief brochure to explain your brand of audio system in the envelope that usually carries the weekly newsletter.

Research shows that envelopes that feel lumpy like there's something inside are usually opened and read. The brochure will talk about the phrase "A penny for your thoughts" and will urge recipients to be in church on Sunday when they will discuss the building campaign after service. Can you find a story that fits? Here's one: The fund-raising committee told of a children's sermon on giving and the Resurrection. The leader asked the kids how long the Resurrection would last, when one of the kids raised their hand and told the whole congregation that "If you get a Resurrection that lasts for 4 hours or more, see your doctor immediately!"

Again, rely on the internet. Enter the words "humorous stories" and "church building campaigns" and you will find much more than you can hope to use. That's why the Narrative is one of the most powerful tactics to use, and it will help you to "Achieve Your Objectives," whatever they might be. Another very powerful everyday persuader is the Testimonial, which has power, value, taste, quality, or any other positive characteristic of a person, product, organization, idea, or practices going for it. Moreover, the Testimony is usually based on the personal experience of the person giving it. As one source puts it, "Good testimonials put potential customers at ease; they reassure the prospect that they're dealing with a real and credible professional or company by outlining the achievable benefits" (http://leahbaade.com/write-persuasive-testimonials-2).

And the critical factor in any such Testimonial is its credibility. Remember back in chapter 2 we looked at synonyms for "credibility." They included such things as trustworthiness, integrity, sincerity, authority, reliability, credibility, and believability. In other words, for this very powerful form of evidence to be persuasive, the testifier must be believable and genuine. That's why so many athletes and celebrities are used in Testimonial advertising. Air Jordan basketball shoes must be best because of whom they are named after (and supposedly designed for). And after all, he could really jump and make slam dunks and score tons of points. And didn't he seem sincere? And reliable? And genuine? All of those things lent to his credibility and made him believable. That's why he sold shoes.

And you could do the same kind of analysis for any Testimonial that you see on television, in magazines, on social media, on billboards, etc. The question for the everyday persuader is "What do I do? Give Testimonials myself or to use Testimonials by others as evidence or proof for my Claims?" There are any number of ways to give Testimonials credibility. Obviously being an expert in a topic is one way. If you are trying to influence a library board, you will want to be sure you have a library card yourself, and you may want to use it as a visual aid—show it to them. Tell them about how much you and your family used the library and in which of its many ways (e.g., books, magazines, newspapers, its web page, video loans, use of their computer and WiFi, its program offerings, its book sales, and others you can learn about). If you've ever been to a library board meeting or been on a library board, mention that.

All of these mean that you have extensive experience with libraries and will build your credibility. If you don't know where it's located, that will destroy your credibility. If you have high qualifications for the proposal you are presenting, mention them. Such things as degrees, years of experience, internships, online courses, other persons who have used your expertise—all help build your credibility and make your Testimonial and your advice to the prospect(s) more persuasive. Taking time for questions obviously helps build credibility, as does a well thought-out and often practiced presentation given with strong delivery technique (http://www.thefreedictionary.com/credibility and http://changingminds.org/techniques/speaking/articles/credibility).

Sometimes it really helps to persuade others if you provide something new and in a memorable way. And you do need to have a specific call to action. Tell your audience what they need to do to improve the situation, and be as specific as you can. Give them handouts with specific steps to be taken and how to measure success. You might also want to give them "freemium" versions of your product (http://blog.slideshare.net/2013/08/19/how-to-build-credibility-with-your-audience/).

You should also be prepared for failure. It's bound to occur at some time that your prospect(s) will refuse to follow your advice, buy your product or service, adopt your organization, vote for your candidate, and so on. Everyone gets rejection sometimes, and what we do and feel in reaction to rejection is what is truly important. How do you handle such rejection—many cannot, you know? They doom themselves to further defeat. First recognize your emotions about your failure and tell about them to a trusted friend or spouse. You might even want to write about them in a diary or a "letter to myself."

Remind yourself that this isn't the most important thing in the world. The sun will still rise in the East and set in the West tomorrow and the day after that. Then take some physical action that accomplishes something—even washing the dishes. It'll help rebuild your confidence. Then try to help someone else or volunteer for something—it'll make you feel good and help you to realize that things could be a lot worse. Finally, try to recount your many past successes, and at the same time do something nice for yourself; give yourself a treat. In Alex Pattakos words "Reject Rejection," and move on to more productive efforts (http://www.huffingtonpost.com/alex-pattakos/dealing-with-rejection_b_3276199).

What sort of script can you use in the face of rejection, because many "failures" can later be turned into successes at a later date? First, thank your prospect(s) for giving you the time to listen to your proposal, and remind them of the points you made. Here's an example:

Persuader: "Well, Mr. Jones, I recognize that you have to make the final decision, but I appreciate you giving me the time to explain my proposal for solving the problem to you, and I hope you'll take another look at the materials I've left with you. You'll recall there are statistics, some typical examples, the stories and testimonials from others who've had similar problems, and the demonstrations that you've seen. If you have any questions about any of this evidence as to the wisdom of my solution and proposal, don't hesitate to call, or if there are other persons who might need further explanation, I can come over and explain.

"The important thing, though, is the big 'Thank You' for your time. I've left my card with you and attached another to the materials left behind as well. Good luck to you whichever proposal you do choose." This sets you up in case Mr. Jones changes his mind after thinking over the things of which you've reminded him. And it gives you a reason to call him after some time—say several weeks—"just to double check" and see if he's changed his mind or to find out which option he finally chooses.

Then you might close with a comment about being glad you met him and that you might stop by in the future with any new products, programs, ideas, etc. that he might be interested in. So ultimately, you may develop success out of initial failure. "Reject Rejection," and you'll succeed in the final analysis.

A subform of Testimony but one of the most credible forms of evidence used to prove one's case is the *Demonstration*. This is because one is able to show the prospect before his or her very eyes the benefits that accrue from the features that your product, brand, organization, proposal, and candidate's features have. As noted above, *Features* and *Benefits* are very similar to the idea of attributes and payoffs that we discussed earlier. It's the fact that the prospect sees, feels, smells, tastes, or hears the difference that these features produce that really involves them. That's why the product demonstration is so often the key tactic used in many television ads.

The classic example of the power of this tactic is the well-known nighttime demonstrations made by Ron Popeil on behalf of his many gadgets initially available only through direct ordering from the Ronco company (e.g., the Vegomatic, the Pocket Fisherman, the Ronco Spray Gun, the Ronco Food Dehydrater, the Ronco Bottle Cutter, and many others). His demonstrations on television are so well known that the names "Ronco" and "Popeil" and the suffix "-O-Matic" as well as the phrases "As Seen on T.V.," "But Wait; There's More," "Operators Standing By," and "Set It and Forget It" have all become iconic in the direct response marketing industry (http://www.biography.com/people/ron-popeil-177863#pop-icon-status).

The power of the demonstration explains the many free samples given away in supermarkets and the test drives always offered by the clever auto salesperson. The prospect becomes involved with the proposal by the demo which stimulates interest, conveys a sense of prospect ownership, answers questions of doubt, and combats consumer concerns, especially if combined with some sort of warrant or guarantee from a trusted source. So if you can, work some kind of demonstration into your everyday persuasion.

TAKEAWAYS

After reading this chapter you should be able to:

1. State Strategies and Tactics for persuading and influencing a given target audience.
2. Define, discuss, and give examples of Aristotle's term *Ethos*.
3. Define, discuss, and give examples of Aristotle's term *Logos*.
4. Define, discuss, and give examples of Aristotle's term *Pathos*.
5. Define, discuss, and give examples of Cicero's term *Invention*.
6. Define, discuss, and give examples of Cicero's term *Arrangement*.
7. Define, discuss, and give examples of Cicero's term *Style*.

8. Define, discuss, and give examples of Cicero's term *Memory*.
9. Define, Discuss and give examples of Cicero's term *Delivery*.

6

USE "SOCIAL PROOF" TO PERSUADE THE PROSPECT(S)

You should note that there is but a single example "Script" included in this chapter. You should, nonetheless, keep the concept of *Social Proof* in mind and use it when you face any challenge of persuading and influencing others. Proof to some folks means things that they can hold, print, show on screens, see, feel, smell, taste, or touch. This would include charts, handouts, slides, graphs, statistical tables, videos of testimonials, free samples, demonstrations or trials, and others. For other persons, proof is dependent on "Who Says So?," "How Do They Know?," "How Smart Are They?," "Are They Credible?," and "How Many of Them Are There?" These are what theorists like Dr. Robert Cialdini call Social Proof.[1] No one likes to be the only person holding a position on what to buy, whom to vote for, what to join, and many other questions. As a result, it's nice to know that very important and highly credible others (and lots of them) feel, believe, and know the same things that you do.

This chapter discusses how and where to find such Social Proof, its types, and how to express it in order to persuade and influence prospects and other audiences that one might want to persuade and/or influence in everyday contexts. His discussion is a little bit different from what we considered in chapter 5 on Evidence and Reasoning. While the knowledge gained there still holds, here we are looking for Evidence and Reasoning that comes from highly credible and strongly/widely believed sources. The evidence and reasoning contained in Social Proof is powerful in the eyes of most prospects and/or audiences.

Cialdini notes the power of this Social Proof in persuasion and influence. Other students of persuasion have called this kind of proof by various names such as the "Bandwagon Effect," "Fashion," "Crowd Effect," "Information Cascades," "Big Mo," "Group Think," "Herd Mentality," "Informational Social Influence," and other names. What these terms basically mean is the tendency in humans to follow the thinking and behavior of highly respected and trusted others.[2]

RECENT EXAMPLES OF THE POWER OF SOCIAL PROOF

The "Housing Bubble" which really began in the late 1990s and ultimately came to a head in 2006–2008 clearly exhibited signs of the "Bandwagon Effect." Potential home buyers were influenced to buy homes by the highly publicized and large profits captured by others who bought, cosmetically improved, and then "flipped" houses and condominiums left and right. In other words, social behavior influenced them to follow suit in hopes of also being able to buy, redecorate and "flip" a house or condo quickly and collect the handsome profits. Of course, record-setting low interest rates made that much easier, especially for persons who might not otherwise qualify for a mortgage. The 2008 market crash and the eight-year recession that followed (the second longest recession in our history behind only the Great Depression) also prompted even lower interest rates but put stringent limitations on what you had to do to qualify for a mortgage. The successes of others prior to the bursting of the bubble were a kind of Social Proof to prospective home buyers and hopeful investors. These eager profiteers then eagerly bought inexpensive homes and condos in hopes of joining the Bandwagon of success. They were victims of the "follow the crowd" error in judgment. In short, Social Proof means the influence of other persons or groups of persons, especially if they are highly respected, friends, and/or well-known or have celebrity status—even negative celebrity status. This is caused by the uncertainty most people feel when making a decision about issues, actions, purchasing expensive products, voting for candidates, joining an organization, and so forth, on their own and without any reassurance from respected others.

UNCERTAINTY IN DECISION MAKING AND THE POWER OF SOCIAL PROOF

The power of Social Proof to persuade and influence others is caused by the uncertainty most people feel when making a decision about issues, actions, purchasing expensive products, voting for candidates, joining organizations, or donating to good causes. We usually don't want to make such important decisions totally on our own and without the advice of respected others. We try to follow the actions of others whom we respect because we assume that they have more and better information, wisdom, and experience than we do.

POLITICS, HORSE BETTING, AND SOCIAL PROOF

For instance, the 2016 GOP presidential field was sent scrambling when Donald Trump, who had never held any political office, entered the already crowded ring using the power of Social Proof. He claimed to "tell it like it is," and in spite of some outrageous policy aims (e.g., for example, if elected, he said that he would deport all Muslims), he garnered a sizable lead over the other sixteen candidates for nomination and had over 25 percent of Republican voters supporting his candidacy for the nomination in early primaries. Then more voters clambered onto his campaign, and the traditional GOP party panicked and sought a well-seasoned candidate who proposed reasonable policies. It was a case of the power of Social Proof. Ultimately, the traditional GOP had symbolically lost, and Trump had *really* won in terms of the electoral college, although the victory came with less than a majority of the popular vote. Nonetheless, it was a victory for his base and a verification of the power of Social Proof.[3] Cialdini gives an example of perceived social influence or proof in horse-race gambling. He pointed out the strategy of not betting initially on the most favored horse that is used by clever gamblers because that would reduce the already low odds offered by the track on that particular horse. Instead, they initially bet small amounts on the horse with the longest odds as that will shorten its odds, but more importantly, it usually causes other potential gamblers to consider doing the same thing. This is because they perceive that others who are "in-the-know" are betting on the long-odds horse for some reason. They think that someone with special "inside knowledge" or experience is placing bets on the long-odds horse. This in turn can cause even more bettors to wager on that horse believing that they too will get in on a good thing. That simply increases the perception of there being a once-in-a-lifetime chance of cashing in on a special bet. Then just before race time, the clever gambler bets on the initially favored horse whose originally low odds will by this time have improved and increased considerably if Social Proof has had its predicted effects.

FIVE TYPES OF SOCIAL PROOF

With the introduction of the internet, email, and Social Media Networks (SMNs) like Facebook, it may even be that using Social Proof is an innovative and new kind of marketing strategy. It's certainly true that SMNs like Facebook can carry lots of persuasive freight. Apparently both the 2016 election and the Brexit vote in the UK were impacted by the "harvesting" of data from a minimum of more than fifty million Facebook individual profiles by a research and consulting firm named Cambridge Analytica (SCL USA).[4] The discovery of the probable impact on both the Brexit vote and the campaign of 2016 vote totals became a scandal.

You can learn about the power of data "harvesting" or "mining" especially when results are cross-referenced with other sorts of data that is readily available from census reports, departments of natural resources, drivers' license departments, and many other data "banks" that exist in our society today. Any search engine will give you details when you enter "Cambridge Analytica" into the search box. Many sources note that there are four types of Social Proof.

Wisdom of the Crowd is the first type of Social Proof which the horse race and betting patterns illustrate, but there are other examples. For instance, periodically I get a report from the electric company telling me that I'm an "over user" in comparison to my neighbors in town. It always makes me feel a little guilty, and I try to be more careful about turning out lights when I leave the room as a result of the frugality of my neighbors. And of course advertisers repeatedly rely on the Wisdom of the Crowd in a way similar to the use of Testimonials discussed back in chapter 5, except that instead of relying on the Testimonial of a single celebrity, athletic star, or well-known movie star, the Wisdom of the Crowd type of Social Proof is usually used by advertisers to say that numerous users—usually in the millions—have already tried the product or are going to vote for the candidate or follow the advice and recommendations of the influential persuader. Cialdini also notes the power of canned laughter in movies, TV comedy, and other venues. The live audience laughs along with the audio-recorded crowd whom it believes "gets" the joke or humor that has been woven into the script.[5] Research shows that the same program with canned laughter consistently outranks its twin without the canned laughter.[6] Social Proof is also similar to Testimonials (see chapter 5) that accompany offers and usually result in increases in sales and/or inquiries. For example, Yelp is checked by 131,000,000 viewers each month to read user reviews about local businesses, and they rate these reviews as generating a positive feeling which lifts sales at usage rate if Facebook also recommends it. It is also the kind of Social Proof that is most likely to "go viral." Recent research shows that without canned laughter, a significant percent of Americans couldn't recognize a good joke in a film or on television without the faked giggles and guffaws.

Expert Social Proof is the kind of proof that influences retail shoppers or persons who are trend followers; for example, you as an everyday persuader who wants to persuade and influence your prospects and other audiences can tap into such types of Social Proof and use it as evidence in your persuasive arguments (see chapter 5). You should now begin tracking what is being said about you, your product, candidate, cause, organization, etc. via some of the various social media now being used.

Get anything relevant on such forums as Facebook, LinkedIn, Google+, and any others online that capture your prospect's attention and interest. Just enter the words "social media" and the topic you are persuading about in any search engine (e.g., "social media candidates" or "social media organizations"). So, it's easy to find resources online—all you have to do is pay attention to SMNs and pick up the news from these businesses (from 5 to 9 percent as a result). In this case, the user reviews serve as Social Proof to convince prospects that the product, service, organization, book, candidate, etc. is well worth purchasing, joining, donating, or voting in its favor.

Celebrity Social Proof is another type of Social Proof that is particularly favored by advertisers, once again in ways similar to the Testimonial, and it claims that the celebrity giving the Endorsement/Testimonial has tried and is believed to still be using the product, brand, donating to the good cause, supporting the candidate, joining the organization, etc. It is estimated that up to 25 percent of television advertisers have used some sort of celebrity Social Proof.

Wisdom of Friends is probably the most effective kind of Social Proof because we naturally trust our friends with whom we probably have a long-term relationship. Moms especially trust the words of their friends and Facebook when shopping, and they are

67 percent more likely to use those two sources of advice than average shoppers, and they have a higher level of confidence about what's trendy.

This also tracks such things as new products, organizations, business growth, consumer traffic patterns, recent statistics about retail spending, various kinds of celebrity ratings on books, music, and movies, any reviews, repeat business, and other indications of social interests or the "crowd effect." Social Proof can also be employed by using other people doing the behavior that you want your prospects to do—like joining, donating, voting, or buying as living examples to whom you can refer. That's why some sales (like those on Black Friday) work so well. Prospective customers see lots of persons going into a particular store, so they also go in naturally. There are several other advantages that can be gained from using such Social Proof. For example, there is little to no investment or budget needed to identify and use Social Proof among organization members, and stakeholders are high-energy volunteers. Some religious evangelists (perhaps even the "great" ones) "salt" the audience with "volunteer" converts (some even with rehearsed Testimonials and even rehearsed cures). After all, don't you think most bartenders "salt" the tip jar?

Don't you think that the "profit" motives of some "Not for Profit" groups are extremely large, especially where the costs go to pay high-priced officers of those so-called Not for Profit organizations? Their actual costs are minimal, and stakeholders might become brand loyal. With non-profit status, you establish relationships that are ongoing with your stakeholders, and for the "For Profit" organizations, you should get more customer ratings, reviews, and/or endorsements.

USING SOCIAL PROOF TO PERSUADE AND INFLUENCE

So, what are some of the ways you gain "social influence" and thus also gain forms of Social Proof with your prospects by using social media to obtain your objectives? Well, we have discussed some of them already, such as doing some research on your target market to learn what might get their attention and interest. But even before that, you need to define your target market. How old are they? What are their basic interests? What do they spend time and money on? In what kinds of activities do they participate? What kinds of organizations do they join? And depending on the market, there are other questions that can be asked. The next step is to develop a website for your product, service, candidate, organization, and the like. Then try to drive prospects to that website through use of printed brochures, business cards, press releases, imprinted items like calendars, free pens, T-shirts, buttons, and the rest. Try any reasonable way to get people there, and then give them a reason to stay at that website of your prospects. You do this by having lots of "buttons" to push to induce the prospect(s) deeper into the website. You want them to push one button such as "Valuable Prize Here" and have that take them to more buttons on the prize page such as one that is labeled "Learn How to Earn Points Here." That one should then lead them to a button labeled "Prize Catalog."

As a result, they go deeper and deeper into the website and learn about the brand, cause, candidate, organization, and so forth. They also are likely to learn more about why others are buying, using, joining, donating, or voting for, and they are ready to try or adopt the product, organization, candidate, service, etc.. Your website might also refer the reader to other Social Proof websites, and they, in turn, may reciprocate. You can also start a blog and place a button to it on your website and use the daily short blog to get users to return to your website and to recommend it to others. Remember, there are viewers of your blog who are unaware of your objectives and/or business.

So, you see the whole idea of Social Proof is to establish a Bandwagon Effect. Also encourage the readers of your website to make comments, to do ratings and/or reviews of it and its objective.[7] Remember that as Cialdini puts it, "One means we use to determine what is correct is to find out what people think is correct. We view a behavior as more correct in a given situation to the degree that we see others performing it." Try to establish or refer to existing uncertainties among prospects, for it is in times of uncertainty or social crisis that we look for social cues from others as to how to behave or what to do.

We now feel dangerous uncertainty over such things as ISIS, North Korean motives, strange weather occurrences, terrorism, theater and school shootings, bombs delivered by remote toy cars or toy drones, and other dangerous groups and/or actions. In such uncertain times, people look around to discover what others are doing. Depending on your prospect's persuasive objective, you may want to urge them to establish a web page for their candidate, product, organization, or cause. Perhaps you could consider using a script like this sample:

Persuader: "Well, I hope I've convinced you that Social Proof is really powerful stuff and that almost anyone like yourself can use it with just a little boost and coaching."

Prospect: "How do you mean?"

Persuader: "Well, it's pretty easy for you to begin now collecting Testimonials from happy patrons, ratings of your group, its offerings, and more and then use these as a basis for starting a web page. If you have succeeded in satisfying a client, ask them if you can use them as a referral or if they'd be willing to write and sign a Testimonial."

Prospect: "How do you get a web page anyway?"

Persuader: "Go onto any search engine and enter the words 'starting a website,' and you'll find many services who will do it for you for free with as little as $1 a month for a domain name and less for hosting. Then you've got to start driving potential voters, joiners, donors, customers to that website using some of the coaching you have just read."

Prospect: "How do you do that?"

Persuader: "Put the website on new business cards, print up some brochures explaining your candidate, business, brand, organization, or cause with plenty of photos with people in them doing interesting things, and get yourself and/or your organization mentioned or listed on as many social media as possible. I'd suggest places like Facebook, LinkedIn, YouTube, Twitter, and others. Enter the words "social media names" on any search engine, and pick one from the listings of the top fifteen or forty names, and you'll be able to search the lists until you find ones that sound right for you and your organization. Then you can explore them by going into their website and try pushing the buttons to learn more about getting prospects deeper into the website. Complete the profiles asked of you there, and emphasize the fact that you have a website and give its address and other social media to which you belong."

"All of these will drive people to your site and will give you further exposure. And be sure to give them steps that they must take by offering a reward to visitors that they can get by pushing a button that takes them on to a deeper level. It could be an opportunity to learn more on the next level and so on. The objective is to keep them there as long as possible, and then use one or more imperative (order giving) action verbs like *Act, Visit, Try, Sign Up, Discover, Attend,* or *Learn.* Also use urgency-stressing words because they are also persuasive. For example, use phrases like *Supplies Limited, While They Last,* or *Two Days Left!*"

Prospect: "Gee, that sounds easy—why doesn't everybody do it?"

Persuader: "They are—and you can be certain that your competition has or will soon be doing it. Check out what and how they do it and borrow from them. Get on it now and you'll be ahead of the rest of your competitors."

Prospect: "Gee that's great! Got any other tips?"

Persuader: "Sure. Check out *50 Expert Tips for Getting Started on Social Media* right now, and use what will work for you— write that address down. It's *50 Expert Tips for Getting Started on Social Media*, and here's another important tip to use when sharing your brand, candidate, cause, or organization. State it in story form for them. Stories and naratives are great proof (see chapter 5) and hold audience attention, everyone likes them, and they usually remember a story better than a statistic. Everyone has a story of how and why they got started and how they want to grow and succeed. Remember, be sure to give the reader a reason(s) for taking action. Rewards always work—use phrases like *Get 40 Percent Off!*, and the word 'Free' is very powerful, as we've said earlier. And don't forget to stress those action steps and action verbs and other action-related words that you want them to remember and to take action on (e.g., *vote, donate, visit, explore, buy,* etc.—almost any action verb will help). Words like *discover, explore, visit, learn, find, meet,* and others are interesting and exciting as well. They tempt me."

Prospect: "Wow!! I'm glad I'm taking notes. You don't have any handout or anything on this, do you?"

Persuader: "Sure, and I'm going to leave it with you at the end, but if I give it to you now you will not pay as close attention to what I have to tell you today. Remember that too and write it down so you don't make the mistake of passing out your hand-out before you get a chance to talk. It'll pull them away from the points you want to make. Let me continue—try to start a conversation via these social media and build a relationship with your potential patron, customer, joiner, or contributor.

Ask any friend who has been using social media successfully for any tips and start small—offer much but expect little. Include visuals or images if you can and use exciting images, especially ones with people in them who are doing out-of-the-ordinary or unusual things like you might see on a ten-second TV commercial—changing a broken automobile windshield, hosting a kid's birthday party, planting a tree, catching a fish, canoeing, and so on. Pictures speak, and especially ones of people doing appealing and fascinating things—but more so if they can also be pinned as reminders to return to your persuasive proposal and think it over."

"KISS is common advice that means 'Keep It Simple, Stupid' and is always a good practice. You don't need to limit yourself to only a few social media, and keep writing that blog we mentioned earlier and include your daily entries on it on your web page. Try to spend some time surfing other social media just to keep up with what things they do. Keep your advice very practical, and use your spell checker everyday—nothing loses a reader quicker than misspellings. Try checking with your local community college and online to discover and take short courses on social media—they'll keep you on the 'cutting edge.'

Prospect: "Geez, I think that's about all I can digest for now. Thanks a million."

Persuader: "Great! What do you want the audience to buy, donate, vote for, join, and so forth because maybe I can help you there too?"

Prospect: "I'll do those things today! Which social media should I use?"

Persuader: "An interesting option to Facebook and its billions of followers (which it resembles to some extent) and some of the other social media sites listed above is Google+ in that it allows you to segment your audience to discover things about them—their interests, ways they spend time and money, activities, and opinions. As a result, you can learn ways to appeal to them, but Google+ allows you to do many other things that can improve your everyday persuasion. Here are a few of them you can use regularly."

During these troubling times when the world seems to be coming apart at the seams, we feel frightened and need support from others. So we search for Social Proof. For instance, during the earthquake of 1989 in San Francisco and right in the midst of the World Series game at Candlestick Park, people in the stands went quiet and stood still, feeling the shifting earth, and then they looked at their neighbors in the seats nearby wondering what those people would do. It's what we all do when we are uncertain—try to establish Social Proof for our actions.[8] That's probably due to scripts from childhood from parents telling us or asking "What are the other kids doing?," "What did the others bring?," or "Did all the kids join in?" We are taught to go along with the herd when in doubt. And when are we usually in doubt? When making decisions regarding what actions we should take at that particular juncture in our lives. We just look around for some verification of what others are doing. Little wonder that Social Proof is such a powerful, everyday persuader. Just look around you for verification. Everyone is interested in what the crowd is doing, so provide them with Social Proof.

TAKEAWAYS

After reading this chapter, you should be able to:

1. Understand and apply the power of Social Proof in your attempts to persuade and influence others.
2. Be able to identify the four types of Social Proof and to be able to use each in your persuasive attempts when appropriate.

3. Know where to look for Social Proof.
4. Understand and know how to access and apply the principles of web page design discussed here.
5. Be aware of the power of SMNs and how to use them for identifying potential prospects while getting yourself known as a person who can persuade and influence.
6. Use SMNs like Google+ and others to segment your audience of prospects and organizations and to promote your skills at persuading and influencing.
7. Use any or all of the thirteen ways to create client loyalty.

7

KEEPING GROUP AND INTERPERSONAL DISCUSSIONS RELEVANT AND "ON TRACK"

Chapter 7 covers the details of conducting a successful meeting with a small group and influencing and persuading them to buy into your proposal. It is really a kind of strategy for persuading and informing others when decisions must be made either by some **formal** group such as a Board of Trustees or by a much more **informal** group such as a Sportsman Club needing to make plans for the sharing of club equipment.

We've all been in formal and informal meetings and/or discussions that seem to go on and on forever without ever getting anywhere—sometimes because of overtalkers or at other times because of complex and thorny issues where everyone wants to have a say. This short chapter will give you a few tips to cut that short and still keep the group remaining on subject. This a key practice for using persuasion and influence, and it's a must for successfully achieving your objectives with your prospects.

THE AGENDA

One of the absolute essential tools for keeping a formal discussion "on track" is a well-planned agenda. It should be thought out ahead of time, with the purpose of the meeting clearly stated, and written in bold at the top of the agenda. Of course, before the meeting really begins to get down to its business, you need to ask group members to add to, subtract from, or change the order of the agenda. Begin with a comment about the rule of following the agenda. That will help prevent irrelevant and "off track" discussion. Also, you should always remind the group that a secretary is taking notes which you'll distribute to all participants later. It also reminds everyone to avoid going off on their own track. If the group does go off on their own track, the leader can simply remind the group with "Hey guys—remember our purpose here is supposed to be finding the organization's best and most economical solution."

RULES OF ORDER FOR THE MEETING/DISCUSSION

Another helpful tool for running a successful discussion of a topic or proposal is an agreed-upon set of rules, the most common of which is *Robert's Rules of Order*. A suggested form for an agenda can be found there also.[1] Meetings should begin with reports by officers and boards. Then old and new business are considered in that order, which allows members to say what they believe the group has already accomplished and what more needs to be completed. They can also add items to the agenda. And *Robert's Rules of Order* can also help with various rules of parliamentary procedure. Keep a copy on hand, and you may want to appoint a parliamentarian. Most people can get a short version, and in an hour or two of reading become sufficiently educated on the most basic things to do like call for a vote, table a motion, make and/or second a motion, how to table a motion, and so on—the basic stuff.

THE PARKING LOT

Another useful tool is what is called a "Parking Lot" and is most useful in informal group discussions and decisions. It is a blank sheet of paper clearly visible to group members with pen or marker next to it. When discussion drifts off track, the leader notes that and says that the tangential topic will be "parked" until later and jots it down. This way nobody feels insulted if their topic doesn't get covered as they would prefer. This fits with the need to follow the agenda and *Robert's Rules of Order*. Also you should have a previously announced time limit for speakers and topics. Keep a large clock, watch, or count down timer on the table in view of all. "The clock has ruled—next speaker" is a good phrase to use in avoiding irrelevant topics or long-winded characters. It also is basically polite and won't hurt anyone's feelings, plus it's useful to keep moving on to the next item on the agenda. A good phrase to use is "Well done—that's a great way to shift to our next agenda item. We're not going to solve this issue during our time today." It's polite and keeps things on track. Keep that up by promising things like "We'll try to reserve enough time allocated in our next meeting to resolve that one. Let's move on." You can see there are many ways to keep moving through the agenda. Other options for continuing include:

1. You might want to try a new topic to start a fresh discussion.
2. Try returning to an old topic.
3. Remind the group that time is running out.
4. You could also promise not to get back to side issues.
5. You can remind the group of how much still needs to be done by meeting's end.
6. Suggest that unless the agenda is finished the group will have to schedule further meetings.

FOLLOW-UP MEETINGS

Sometimes the issues haven't been fully discussed at the end of
the time set for adjournment. Ask, "When can we meet again?"
Nobody wants that. You could also try "What day of the week is
best for meetings?" Most formal meetings do require follow-ups
which you really should establish before adjournment.

INFORMAL MEETINGS

Remember that there are meetings where there is no agenda—
only a general topic which is discussed among only a few persons.
Examples include counseling situations between a parent and a
child, the boss and an employee or a group of employees, between
salespersons and prospects, between candidates and groups of vot-
ers or maybe a single voter, between two neighbors disagreeing
over property rights, or between a minister and a member of the
congregation. Keep such interactions relevant and on track even
when the topic is extremely emotional. It may not even have a
specific goal. It could just focus on the consideration of ideas,
issues, or policy. It may not end up with a specific product at all—
it could just end without any controversy. Naturally, such discus-
sions are very informal. There is no agenda, and *Rules of Order*
don't exist except that you would expect everyone to be civil with
one another. There is no true leader in such meetings, though
someone might facilitate the flow of conversation. A typical topic
might revolve family hassles (e.g., the use of the family summer
cottage) and how they can be avoided, problems to solve, and
conclusions to be reached. Everyone should have an opportunity
to speak openly and disagree with others in the group. Everyone's
commentary may be either positive, negative, or just to check on
the agreement's details. The discussion can be spirited if everyone
feels they are working together to reach a satisfactory conclusion.

FACILITATING DISCUSSION FLOW

The facilitator should mention these goals frequently and continuously reinforce statements and feelings of unity of purpose. The facilitator should stress that there is a time to adjourn. Be willing to admit that you are wrong or that there are multiple okay points of view, as in "I guess I probably speak in my own interests and could be wrong given what some have expressed." Be sure that others have a chance to disagree and express their side of the issue. Keep the overtalkers from monopolizing, and encourage the under talkers to speak up. A script like this would help: "David, that position is clear but I'm not sure how Elizabeth feels about the issue. Elizabeth, what do you think?" Remember no one is living in the other person's mind, and some of the others might want to say more. Before transitioning to a new subtopic, say something like "Are we done with this part of the discussion or do some of you want to say more on it?" If everyone is to be satisfied, the meeting should reach a productive conclusion with the promise that actions are going forward. Try using a concluding summation like this: "What do you want the next actions to be? Who should take those actions, and what is the timetable for them?" Record the responses in your "Parking Lot" and distribute the answers to all group members. Publicize all the answers wider to all employees, invited participants, and others. These are just a few of the things one can do to help keep meetings on track, but there are occasions when, while there is progress being made, conflict raises its ugly head. Two members disagree on a topic, or on an interpretation of the situation or piece of evidence, and suddenly progress ceases.

TAKEAWAYS

After reading this chapter, you should be able to:

1. Be able to create an agenda for a meeting using the traditional order of the day.
2. Use *Robert's Rules of Order* and appoint a parliamentarian to keep the group on track.
3. Understand and employ a "Parking Lot" in meetings which you chair.
4. Know how to use certain phrases and tactics to keep groups which you chair "on track" in their deliberations.
5. Know how to discourage overtalkers and encourage undertalkers.
6. Know how to facilitate discussion flow in meetings which you chair.
7. Be able to move groups to specific actions to be taken and to make them aware of future meetings and topics to be considered.

8

BUILD YOUR OWN CREDIBILITY

Pointing out your accomplishments regarding the aims you hope to reach is one powerful way to make prospects believe you and to be influenced to adopt your suggested actions, proposals, offers, invitations, etc. Such things as past successes, special training, having taken advanced classes, and testimonials about you as an influential persuader from former satisfied clients are all examples of this kind of building one's own credibility. You should tell your prospects about your reputation and invite them to call previous customers or clients to get referrals.

Try to heighten your expertise in regard to the problems being addressed by your prospects. Compare your accomplishments with competitors of lesser skill, expertise, and success. Show that you are to be believed because of your character and past record as well as by the evidence shown from outside sources and the Testimonials from your referrals from other times and places. Many professionals keep a three-ring binder full of Testimonials by previous clients to have on hand when meeting with a prospect for the first time. It's not really difficult to do, and as long as you are proud of your work and get complimented on it, it makes sense to keep a record of those achievements.

Why is it that we almost automatically will believe some persons and not others? Are we equipped at birth with an instinct to believe persons with certain physical characteristics like height, weight, ease of movement, or facial expression? Or are there identifiable techniques or tactics that you can use to make yourself believable or credible? We noted earlier that the word "credibility" carries a lot of connotations with it, as you can see when you look it up in the thesaurus. Some synonyms for "credibility" are *trustworthy, reliable, integrity, authority, good-standing, sincere, believable, accurate, respectable, expertise, dependable, honest, responsible, knowledgeable, faithful, steadfast, authentic, convincing, plausible,* and *above board.* Those are all the kinds of things that influence and hence will persuade others, so if you want to be successful at getting others to buy, vote, join, contribute, volunteer, change their attitudes, values or behaviors, and so forth, you must work on building and developing your credibility. Let's just assume that almost every person starts life with zero credibility. Then how do they develop credibility that influences others and can thus persuade them?

Well, one simple thing is to always show up and on time or a little early, as promised. That helps develop an image of *reliability*—another synonym for credibility. And if you are meeting with a group, be sure to get there early so you can check the layout for the meeting and any audio-visual equipment you hope to use. And extra time is good to meet a few early arrivals and introduce yourself to them and also ask them questions about themselves. Ask about their family, their job, their hobbies or interests. Another thing people need to do is to develop some kind of expertise at some outside skill, set of experiences, or field of endeavor that doesn't relate exactly to your proposals or offers (e.g., carpentry, medicine, fishing, cooking, gardening, or the legal system). That takes being *knowledgeable,* which is another of those synonyms for credibility. Becoming *knowledgeable* requires study, learning, practice, repeated practice, and remembering the elements of the field of endeavor in which we want to be credible and conversant. And knowing that you are knowledgeable about a variety of things helps to build your credibility. It means that you are certainly knowledgeable about the issue under consideration and that your recommendations are also credible.

Most persons would equate credibility with really believing in what you say—no half measures or faking beliefs. That's why the word "sincere" is in the list of synonyms or equals for "credibility." It has an interesting history as a word. In the Latin, the prefix "sine" means "without" and the root means "wax." The combination of the two into "sine-cere" was meant to refer to marble carvers of the pillars that stood in front of temples. The dishonest pillar carver would camouflage or hide his mistakes by covering them over with wax that was tinted to match the marble of the pillar. Only years later would the wax fall out, exposing the by-now absent pillar carver—like a false friend.

Repeatability is another byword for credibility, and by it we mean that the influential persuader can be counted on for holding the same opinion today as they did yesterday and that they will tomorrow unless there is a very good reason for changing. For example, following the Japanese attack on Pearl Harbor, people changed their opinions about the country's position from a neutral one to one of being an ally of the UK overnight.

More recently, we saw an unusual and bizarre string of extreme weather (i.e., category 4 and 5 hurricanes, extremely hot and dry summers, rising sea levels, flooding, droughts, and rare tornados). The reality of climate change caught people's attention, and they were concerned that the strange events might be repeated again and again in the future. Repeatability is another touchstone for credibility in the scientific method of research. If your experiment cannot be repeated with the same results from day to day, there's good reason to believe that something else other than what you think causes a given effect. Something else is actually the true cause of the observed effect.

Credibility is not so easy to pin down. In fact, it's an elusive concept and defies easy definition. As a result, giving advice as to how one can build up their own credibility is somewhat risky. The advice I give here helps build credibility *in some cases,* but not in all cases. What follows is sound advice on how to build one's credibility in most cases, so here goes:

1. Refer to one's own past record of achievements and stands on issues. This is almost always a powerful credibility builder. In our culture, one's "permanent record" is the best indication of our credibility. We have always been reminded of this from grade school and afterward. When applying for a job, for college, to join many organizations, and in a multitude of ways, our past history is an indication of our credibility and a reliable sign of our future behavior in similar situations. The collection of Testimonials from previous users of your services also serves as a bulwark to your credibility.

2. Politicians frequently refer to their past record of legislation during previous terms of office, noting things like the number of bills they have sponsored or co-sponsored, their record of regular attendance, case studies of their assistance for various members of their constituency, and so forth. All of these demonstrate that they are dependable and reliable—all synonyms for credibility.

3. Tradespeople do the same when they refer to the number of years of experience they have, their efforts to improve skills of carpentry, electricity, concrete finishing, and so forth through attendance at things like short courses/workshops, and their pursuit of advanced certificates. All of these indicate that they are in good standing and can be relied upon.

4. Businesses build their credibility by including in their advertising, sales literature, and even on their billing invoices things like years that they have been in business, accident-free workdays, membership in professional societies, customer satisfaction survey results, sponsorship of community-minded events, and other indices of excellence.

5. Professionals like physicians, lawyers, dentists, and various types of therapists do many of the things that businesses do (e.g., mention years of experience, memberships in professional societies, or being licensed by professional associa-

tions like the AMA and so on). Again, these are indications of being knowledgeable, members in good standing in their profession, dependable and therefore credible, and that their advice can be depended upon.

So, you can see that citing one's accomplishments or the "permanent record" of our personal and professional lives helps to cement one's credibility in the minds of our clients, customers, the audience, voters, members of an organization to which we belong, and others as well. That provides you with one additional way to build your credibility, and that will influence others and will ultimately help persuade them to support your brand, candidate, your contributors, your volunteers, the organizations or worthy causes that you recommend, and more.

Another credibility-building technique or tactic is to cite evidence that supports the position or point that we are trying to make. Even better at developing our credibility is if this evidence comes from a highly respected person, professional society, association, scholarly organization, or other type of organization which specializes in or about what we do (e.g., "He's the founder of that Artificial Intelligence Think Tank corporation). Recall what we said in chapter 6 about Social Proof. Audiences initially have at least a neutral feeling about a persuader's credibility. It helps when you can bolster that neutral feeling with famous and highly credible sources who are well known for their expertise, trustworthiness, and credibility. By citing such respected and perhaps even famous experts, your own credibility is furthered.

Maybe the targets become even a little bit more positive toward you as a person who can be trusted and believed. Otherwise, why would they take the time to even listen to you? Human beings are confirmation-seeking creatures. Your audience doesn't like being unsure. They don't like having doubts. So, when you quote or refer to highly credible sources as your proof or evidence, also tell your prospects/audience why your sources are highly credible (e.g., "She is CEO of a billion dollar research firm"). This builds your credibility, and it shows that you don't just use any old source to prove a point. Also, when you accompany that evidence with non-verbal cues of honesty and believability, it helps them feel more certain, more believing, and less doubtful. All of those things make your audience feel more psychologically comfortable because you have confirmed what they initially thought and later wanted to believe. They trust and like you now. That is what they wanted to feel.

You see, you have begun to develop *Rapport* with them. And Rapport with the audience is another key factor in *Building Your Own Credibility.* When we have Rapport with others they believe that we are like them. We share with them things like opinions, values, and beliefs, and can therefore be trusted and depended upon to give wise advice and counsel.

Another thing you can do to develop your own credibility is to offer to assist your audience in some way. One of the most frequently used and simplest ways is to provide free information to the audience. If you have been doing a good job of audience analysis, you are probably aware of their needs. These are usually the everyday problems that arise in a complicated and complex digital society. "How do you develop a web page and should you?," "Why spend a lot of time writing a blog?," "Who read blogs?," "Can I use email to pay bills?," "Is it at all dangerous?," "Can I use email to communicate with my relatives in another country?," and "Do libraries offer courses in how to use spreadsheets at tax time?" The answers to all of these questions can be easily included on your web page via FAQs or "Frequently Asked Questions," which is a list of questions next to a button that the consumer or audience can press. This takes them to a list of questions that others have frequently asked in the past and which can be expanded on as new queries arise. The user simply presses the number next to the question that they have and—*presto*—the answer appears, and the user can exit the web page or go back to the list of queries and see if there are other FAQs to which they want the answers. And as noted, the list can be expanded as your new queries come in. There's a space at the bottom of the list for the user to jot down their unanswered questions.

You can see how this helpful device can be to the everyday person just trying to get along in a complex world. And at the same time that you are providing free help to the user, you are also *Building Your Own Credibility*. This device of FAQs can be included on your web page, so if you don't already have a web page, put developing one or having an expert at building web pages at the top of your "To Do" list.

Another way to build your own credibility is to develop a wide range of interests in and knowledge about various sports, activities, organizations, issues of the day, and so on. This will prevent you from being tongue-tied upon meeting a potential persuadee, prospect, or audience member. You can always ask them, "What are some of the things that interest you and that you're involved in—like activities or organizations?" This gives them an opening for continuing the conversation, and depending on how widely and deeply you have researched them and become knowledgeable about the things that they are interested in, you will be able to impress them during the continuation of the conversation, and this will help to build your credibility further.

We like to believe persons who are like us and have the same interests indicates this kind of sameness. They will believe you or rate you as a good and credible source if they feel that you are sincerely like them. Zig Ziglar, the famous communications consultant and lecturer, once said, "People don't care about how much you know, until they know how much you care." And having similar interests usually indicates a significant level of caring. So, develop a wide and deep knowledge of and interest in many things—activities, interests, organizations, current events, and more. Be sincere or "Without Wax," and you'll be more successful and believable at persuading and influencing others. In short, you'll be building credibility.

An immensely effective tactic for developing credibility is to work at building a level of reciprocity with your prospects or audience (see chapter 4). You began this process if you offered something of value to your prospects or audience, like the answers to FAQs, because then it will be difficult to develop reciprocity with the users. If you're clear about not wanting something from them, just be patient because it's likely that they'll indeed offer something in return. It won't be just because you asked for it. It would be just like someone saying, "Aren't you going to thank me for opening the door for you?"

It's always reassuring when people don't behave as if they "know it all" and are willing to admit some level of weakness or vulnerability. Animals do this when they first encounter another like them, such as a dog meeting another dog for the first time. They inspect the other and allow the other to inspect them, and even in battle they will offer a potential foe for their throats. It is important to compare what you have to offer to the competition's offerings and to admit any weaknesses you have beforehand. It indicates that you are trustworthy (after all, you admitted to a small weakness), responsible, and believable.

Here it is useful to use those Testimonials from past users of your brand, service, organization, candidate, political party, church, and so on to support your case for being the option selected. Testimonials are frequently used in religious attempts to influence and persuade others. When the preacher claims to have the power to eternally save sinners, it's always useful to have the audience listen to a person who has been saved. As a result, the audience listens to that Testimony from such saved souls before being asked to come forward and also be converted. Testimonials are also useful in the law where they help to persuade the judge and/or the jury that the defendant is either innocent or guilty.

Advertisers often use the Testimonials of previous users of the brand, service, organization, etc. who testify as to their positive experience with the advertised product or brand. Sometimes, their mere presence as a spokesperson for the product or brand is enough to influence and persuade consumers to purchase. Consider Wheaties. Its box usually has a picture of a famous athlete on it together with the brand's famous slogan "Wheaties: The Breakfast of Champions!" The box, spokesperson, and the familiar slogan all work together to influence and persuade the customer. Another example is the degree to which Michael Jordan has been able to convince his audience of the brand of athletic shoe to buy and use. Sometimes just ordinary-seeming persons give convincing Testimonials about products and brands in the areas of one's appearance or what to use when wanting to treat some health problems such as plaque psoriasis.

It is curious how much people seem to enjoy and respect both the good story and the talented storyteller. It's what has made for the great stand-up comics of show business across time from the days of the silent movies and onward. Memorable storytellers have always had high credibility and have been influential and persuasive even when their material was not comic but instead was deadly serious.

Reinforce your already developed credibility by utilizing the power of the story or the narrative in presentations to prospects/ audiences. This is a skill that seems to just come naturally to some persons, but it is a skill that can be learned by anyone willing to take the time to discover good material and then to rehearse presenting it in enjoyable and influential and persuasive ways. Just try to listen to some of the TED stories on public radio sometimes. You don't need hundreds and hundreds of great stories—a dozen or fewer suffices to augment one's growing credibility. The internet is a good place to load your holster. Just enter a word like "Irish," followed by "mother-in-law," "drunk," or "lawyer" followed by the word "jokes" and you'll find more than you can use. The Bible teaches us to be willing to "go the extra mile for others," and they'll always remember and respect you for it—another level of credibility.

The word "respectable" is one more of the synonyms for credibility. It's easy to think about being comfortable believing someone whom you respect, especially if they are also memorable for doing more than is required or expected of them. So, it's useful to think of this biblical admonition about the extra mile when dealing with your audience. Ask yourself and them if possible, "Is there anything more that I can do to help you?" Just asking the question is usually sufficient in raising your credibility in their eyes. It signifies that you do really care about their welfare, and remember what Zig Ziglar said about caring. It's a low-effort and low-cost thing to do and will lend greatly to your credibility. Your prospects and audiences want to know how much you care. Your ability to persuade and influence those others that you want to buy, vote, join, commit, donate, believe, etc. depends on what they think you care about—them and their concerns or your own objectives. Your credibility will grow if you care about your audience.

Listening is one of the least studied and probably the most important subject taught in our schools today.[1] Just think about it. How many years in the grade, middle, and high school did you study the importance of reading and writing? Most of you will say twelve, and that's the way it's been since I was a kid too. But research shows that about 80 percent of one's business day is spent in one of four verbal forms of communication—reading, writing, speaking, and listening. Where does that last one fit in, and how might it affect your credibility? Writing accounts for but 9 percent of that time; reading accounts for another 16 percent of our communication time; speaking tallies up to about 30 percent of our verbal communication day; and listening accounts for the final 45 percent of our verbal communication day. It's *the* most important verbal communication skill, and yet it is the one that's least taught in our schools. No wonder that we sometimes have low credibility ratings when tested on how much comprehension we have when tested just a few minutes after listening to a lesson, a speech, a lecture, or a sermon.

To tell the truth, we are basically terrible listeners, and it hurts our credibility to no end. If your prospect thinks that you aren't listening to them as they tell you of their problems—the ones they want your help in solving—then how good do you think your advice is to them? If you're truly interested in building your credibility, one of the most important things you can do is to improve your listening skills. There are a variety of short courses available at your local library, community college, and online. Here are some of the cues to good listening that your prospects/audience will notice as they talk.

- Maintain Eye Contact: When you are looking someone in the eye, you have no choice but to pay attention. There's no question that you are paying attention.
- Don't Interrupt the Speaker: Save your questions/comments until the speaker finishes.
- Sit Still: Fidgeting suggests that you aren't really paying attention.
- Nod Your Head: This indicates to the speaker that you're taking in the information.
- Attend to Non-Verbal Cues: Paying attention to what the speaker *doesn't* say is just as important as what s/he does say. Look for various types of non-verbal cues such as facial expressions, gestures, vocal volume and tone, and posture.
- Repeat Instructions and Ask Appropriate Questions: Once the speaker has finished presenting his/her speech, repeat the specific directions or instructions that you've just heard.
- Lean toward the Speaker: You will appear to be paying attention, and you probably are.

So, there you have some helpful advice about how listening really can help you build your own credibility, and that credibility will make you more influential and persuasive with others.[2]

There are certain words in the English language that are more influential and persuasive than others. These are powerful words and should enhance your credibility if you use them regularly in your presentations: *You, Money, Save, Results, Health, Easy, Love, Discovery, Apply, Proven, New, Safety,* and *Guarantee.* There are also a raft of words that are especially impressive and credibility-augmenting in the worlds of sales and marketing. Hogan and Speakman list them in their book, *Covert Persuasion.* They are: *Free, Yes, Fast, Why, How, Secrets, Sale, Acclaimed, Amazing, Authentic, Breakthrough, Classic, Announcing, Compare, Unlimited,* and *Surprising.*[3] Experiment with working some of these "Power Words" and "Sales/Marketing Words" into your presentations and see how they work as influencers and as persuaders. Try to determine if these words have boosted your credibility if you can.

Getting the prospect/audience involved in your building credibility is powerful. Do it by asking them questions and then following up on their answers in some way. Questions have a variety of types of topics. For example, there are questions about preferences. You might ask, "If you have to choose between a new job in Alaska or a new job in New York, how would you go about learning what life was like for persons in each state?" or "What makes you decide for whom you will vote in your local elections?" Then there are questions about experiences persons have or have not had, such as "Have you ever had to fire someone, and how did you do it, and did you feel O.K. about it once it was done?" or "What do you think you would do if your stock portfolio doubled in a year?"

Then there are many almost philosophical questions you could ask, like, "What direction do you think your company is heading?," "What would you do to influence that direction?," "What do you believe your prospects think about the future in terms of their jobs?," "Why do some people have so much difficulty deciding between various options?" Try to use the following script in your opening words: "Here is how and why I feel about this troublesome problem or issue that we're trying to straighten out. I believe that this is a problem that we can solve." This gives you ownership of your feelings and doesn't lay blame anywhere, and it gives the feeling that you are sincerely trying to work as a team. The words "we can straighten it out" are also helpful versus words suggesting that somebody else is going to win instead.

Asking questions lets your prospects/audience know that you are truly interested in them and their opinions and feelings. The questions demonstrate that you *do really care* about what they think, feel, and fear. And credibility helps influence and persuade your prospects to make important decisions—the focus of chapter 9—"Move to a Decision."

TAKEAWAYS

After reading this chapter, you should be able to:

1. Build a collection of written Testimonials describing how your services are superior to that of competitors. This will be influential and persuasive to new prospects/audiences.
2. Arrive early for group appointments and be knowledgeable enough on a variety of topics to be able to socialize with members of the group who have also arrived early.
3. Practice Sincerity or being "Without Wax" when relating to others whom you hope to influence and persuade.
4. Cite your past record of accomplishments to prospective audiences, organizational representatives, clients, etc.
5. Cite the professional organizations to which you belong, and also cite your record of accomplishments on behalf of those organizations.
6. Use Social Proof in and on a variety of situations to help build your credibility.
7. Develop Rapport with prospects and/or audiences by telling them of your opinions, beliefs, and values.
8. Begin to develop your own web page by yourself or by using the services of an expert web page designer, and be sure to include FAQs that relate to the objectives you hope to reach.
9. Begin to develop a level of Reciprocity with your prospective clients and/or audiences.
10. Be a better listener by practicing good listening habits like maintaining good eye contact with those communicating to you, asking questions of them, nodding your head while they communicate, sitting still or leaning toward them in your seat or while standing, and maintaining a professional posture and attitude while listening to their message.
11. Be able to openly admit your minor weaknesses when compared with the competition.

12. Develop a repertoire of enjoyable and sometimes humorous narratives or stories that carry an important lesson in the issue under consideration.

13. Use some of the "Power Words" and "Sales Marketing Words" noted by Hogan and Speakman in your proposals, advice, and counsel to prospects and/or audiences whom you want to influence and persuade.

14. Use the tactics of asking questions and frequently asking follow-up questions to show your interest in the issue under consideration and that you really do care about your prospects and/or audiences.

15. Ask your prospects and/or audiences some of the more philosophical questions noted above in order to determine their deeper feelings and experiences to focus on the problems that they are experiencing.

9

MOVE TO A DECISION

It is always difficult to make a decision because we are afraid we will be wrong. Then we will be blamed and perhaps will suffer major losses (e.g., our job, a promotion, a raise, etc.). The everyday persuader needs to convince the prospect(s) that not to make a decision is a decision in itself. That gives them professional and effective reasons to move to a certain and preferred decision.

This chapter presents the influential persuader with several models or ways of decision making that are common sense advice for making a decision, such as: "Sleep on it." "Consider yourself as an advisor trying to tell a friend what to do, make a spreadsheet of advantages and the disadvantages of your decision," and more. We see a dramatic example of decision making in Shakespeare's *Hamlet*. Hamlet asks, "To be or not to be, that is the question," as he tries to make *the* most difficult decision of his young life—whether to commit suicide or not. He has learned from his father's ghost that his father's brother (Hamlet's uncle) has secretly murdered his brother—Hamlet's father and king at the time of the murder. Hamlet's uncle has also declared himself king by also quickly wedding the deceased king's widow (Hamlet's mother and the queen). This bothers Hamlet a great deal. It is a clear case of regicide (killing a royal person), and Hamlet is thus a potential murder victim also as he is the heir apparent to the throne of Denmark (next in line to become king when he becomes of age). He is also honor bound to avenge his father's murder. Thank goodness none of us or your prospects/audience will have to make such a decision. However, your prospects/audience will have to decide about your proposals and/or your advice.

DECISION MAKING IS A PROCESS

Remember that decisions don't usually occur all at once in a given instant. Rather, decisions occur in a series of steps or stages across time—sort of like a recipe, a formula, a procedure, or an *algorithm*, to use a fancy computer programming term. Initially, you really never know where your prospect is in any of those stages, so the first thing to do is just to ask them questions about the upcoming decision that needs to be made by them. If you understand which stage of the process they are in, you'll help them in making that decision, and being helpful will help you persuade and influence them and their ultimate decision.

Let's use the purchase of a piece of real estate for an example—a home in this case. The first stage in that process is usually deciding to purchase rather than rent—the exact place to purchase usually comes later. So, a good question to ask is where, when, how, and why the person whom you are trying to persuade made that first stage in the decision. The following script would work fine: "I remember first deciding that it would be better to buy rather than rent." "When did you make that decision, and what made you decide to look into buying a place of your own instead of paying rent, and what made you decide to look?" Then you need to let the person explain. It's because that allows them to engage in "self-persuasion," which is very powerful. Reinforce their explanation by saying things like "Yes, that's what we thought too" or "Yup. Those rent receipts bothered us too" or "We wanted to have more space too and to build value and equity for the future." By having to explain how they got to this first step or stage one in the decision process and by hearing it reinforced, your prospect or audience will take *Ownership* of the decision process. That important stage happens because now it's their idea and not yours. That makes moving to the next branch in this "Decision Tree" a lot easier.

THE DECISION-MAKING TREE

Yes, decision making is like a tree with various branching possibilities from which your prospect or audience can and must finally choose. You can influence and persuade them along the way again by asking more questions. For example, you might ask, "Did you decide you wanted to buy into a piece of rental property or a stand-alone single-family home instead, and why did you decide to make your choice?"

Focusing the Decision

There are two very important words in that question, and they are "decide" and "home," as they imply that at least a part of the final decision has already been made, and also the word "home" makes one feel comfortable—maybe even cozy and familiar with the property. Stage two in the decision-making process or Tree is *Focusing* the decision, and your prospect or audience may already have taken it, but if you're already asking the question again, it reinforces their decision. Let's suppose they respond that they want to buy a stand-alone single-family home. It's time to move to stage three in the Decision Tree—narrowing the decision.

Narrowing the Decision

This is a *Narrowing* of the focus of the decision. Once again, it is eased by asking a question. Perhaps you could ask, "What sort of neighborhood would you like for your *home* to be located—the city or a suburb?" Usually, restricting the choice to just two options is best. If you asked them instead if they would like city, rural, suburban, or urban, you'd probably introduce an option they hadn't even considered, and they would have to backwater and re-think things which would just slow down the decision-making process. That's not always the best thing to do. It's much more comforting for the prospect to feel that things are moving along as nice, orderly, and reasonably as they'd hoped. Suppose they've emphatically answered "suburban." Then it's time to go on further in the Decision Tree branches by moving to stage four of the process—concentrating the decision.

Concentrating the Decision

Concentrating their decision is important and can be helped by a question such as "Did you have any idea about which suburbs?" Again, suppose they answer naming two or three similar suburbs. You are very much further along the decision-making process, and it's time to move to stage five of the process, or the *Taking Action* step, and it's the most likely point in the process to result in a sale, vote, commitment, donation, recruitment to a church or another organization, etc.

Taking Action

The prospect/audience is as ready to follow your advice as they ever will be. Remember that your prospect or audience feels lots of stress and maybe even anxiety over making this decision, and he/she instinctively knows that Taking Action will end those feelings. Most decision makers report that they have feelings of great relief, ease, and sometimes excitement because now they concluded their decision and took action on it—they have cemented its permanence, at least for the present. Humans have a basic need for these feelings of tranquility. Tell them that you're sure they've made a wise decision. That's reinforcement to them.

Reinforcing the Decision

It's often useful at this time to remind your prospect/audience what it would have been like had they decided to delay making the decision and therefore not taking any action. Perhaps interest rates would have gone up. Maybe another buyer, whom they hadn't known about, was almost ready to make a higher offer to the seller. Then the search process would have to be initiated all over again. The stress and anxiety would return, the worry about the many "What if?" questions, would still be there, and so on. Urging them to imagine what that would have been like will "seal the deal" and reinforce the correctness of the decision in their mind. Decision making also relates to how much the individual wants to risk. It's extremely valuable for you, the persuader, to get some idea of how much their prospects/audience want(s) when proposing something that will result in change. People want things to be stable and predictable.

Social scientists call this "resistance to change," and it's useful for the influential persuader to have some idea of how to overcome this resistance. Hogan offers two easily recalled methods. One is to make your offer more attractive than what the competition is offering and more attractive than what no change would be like. The other option to overcoming the resistance to change is to emphasize the negative things that can result from not changing or following the competition's advice.[1] In the real estate purchase decision, interest rates could go up or another party could make a better offer and get the property from under you.

A decision which I recently had to make followed these same steps. It was related to my heating and cooling contractor. Our furnace had been acting up and was not responding to sudden changes in temperature properly. He explained that it was sixteen years old, and we had put it in partially because our old furnace back then was only 70 percent efficient. Now, the replacement furnace was acting up too. A new replacement would be 90 percent efficient. As a result, there was a great savings in our heating and cooling costs. He said that the industry predicts that the average life of a furnace is about seventeen years, and probably the reason it was acting up was because the computer board got wet from condensation. He'd replace the computer board for about $400, but there was no telling what would go next. And an entirely new furnace costs $3,400, but a tax rebate is available. He said he could put in a brand new 96 percent efficient furnace for about $3,000 and would throw in a $250 programmable thermostat. So, there was my decision, and it involved some risk in one option (fixing the old furnace), but there was a significantly higher initial cost but much lower risk with the other option. It would have been a tough choice fifteen years ago, but we had enough savings put aside for emergencies like this one, so that really helped in the decision-making process. I recommend it to everyone. It was a cool mid-September day that reminded you that winter wasn't that far off. Who wanted to have furnace problems when it was a blizzard or minus ten degrees outside? It was a cinch. I didn't have to go through the first five stages in decision making, and so I just took action—stage five of the Decision Tree. We've had the same heating and cooling contractor for quite a few years now, and his brand of furnace is highly reputable. Trying to outguess the averages of getting a reliable heating and cooling contractor or a business partner(s) is usually a poor way to make decisions—especially the emotional and difficult ones like getting married, divorced, going into business, and so on. So, don't worry over such decisions until you have to make one.

Research the Decision

Hogan believes that once you've done your research you'll have a greater chance of making a better decision than the other person who puts it off for months. In other words, don't borrow trouble by waiting until action is essential. If you want people to follow your advice, urge them to take action now—their attitudes usually follow. If you're asking for significant change, try to change the prospect's environment—go out for coffee and a doughnut. Another thing to remember about decision making is that when there is a risk of losing something, most people fear losing more than they want to win. It's great to come out on top, but it's absolutely unacceptable to come out on the bottom. I know that doesn't sound rational, but no one said that people are rational when they make decisions—especially the emotional ones. And if there are a lot of options, people freeze and can't make any decisions.

ADVICE FOR HELPING YOUR PROSPECT OR AUDIENCE MAKE DECISIONS

Ask Lots of Questions

As you are trying to persuade and influence your prospect or audience, ask questions that will help you determine what their default position might be. For instance, you could ask, "Have you ever had to make a decision similar to this or of this magnitude?" or "In past decisions like this one, what most helped you determine which way to choose?" or "If you were giving advice to someone who had to make a decision like this one, what would it be like?" You are really attempting to cover stages or steps one, two, three, and four of the Decision Tree model we discussed above. You are helping them with *Taking Ownership, Focusing, Narrowing,* and *Concentrating* as you continue with more and more probing questions, and hopefully you're reinforcing their decision. And all the while, you are conducting a very sophisticated audience analysis that reveals your prospect or audience's default position(s) because your target may have more than one default position. Another thing to keep in mind as you influence your prospect is that most choices in decision making involve some level of risk. As noted earlier, most people fear losing far more than they hope to win, unless the decision is "rigged" for them to win, and even in some rigged decisions the long-term results might be negative or a big failure or loss.

Risk and Saving Face

Persons winning the lottery frequently experience major problems, family and otherwise, following the awarding of the prize. So, risk is an integral element in any decision making, and the fear of loss always lurks in the background, no matter how certain the outcome. Remind them of how better off they are after having followed your advice. Sometimes you are going to have to find a way for your prospect to save face. Dale Carnegie advised the same thing years and years ago.[2] A good way for you to help the prospect to save face is to suggest that there are possible outside (even conspiratorial) forces in play. Say something like "I'm sorry that things didn't work out perfectly for you on that decision to _____, but who could have even guessed that _____ would happen and change all the predictions that _____. But look at it this way, what you have gained in knowledge about the technology to _____, and it will make you a leader in the field of _____." The topic or area of interest being talked about doesn't matter. It could be postal rates, oil prices, computers, self-driving cars, or amusement parks. Try any of those topics in the *Save Face* script I've just given you. With a few adjustments and clever word choices, you'll see how it provides an *escape clause* for just about any mistake, wrong decision, and loss that happens.

Framing the Decision

Another critical factor in moving to a decision is *Framing*, or the ways in which information needed for the decision is presented.[3] We dealt with this earlier when we considered two ways to *frame* the price/value of ground beef. As a result, you need to be very careful about how you *frame* the options involved in the decision, so consider carefully your choice of words and phrases. Again, the best way to proceed is by asking your prospect(s) or audience questions about how they feel, and depending on how they feel, help them make this decision. If the target wants more information, get it; if they would appreciate advice in deciding, give it; and respond in similar ways for other and similar questions about making decisions.[4]

Phrases That Help

Here are a few sample phrases that you might try depending on the situation and the audience analysis you've done as your target is moving through the decision stages. So with the situation and the nature of the decider in mind, here goes: "You might want to . . . ." "What if this were to personally affect you and your family?" "Are you interested in asking . . .?" "If you could have everything your own way, what would it be?" "What will things be like if you make no decision?" "Would it surprise you that eighty percent of . . .?" "Would you like more data?" I don't know if you've considered . . . ." "How do you usually make decisions?" "What cues lets you know that . . .?" Why does Mr. Z disagree with you so much?" "You know that it isn't absolutely necessary for you to . . . ." "Some people in the industry think . . . ." "Have you ever tried something similar before?" "What resulted?" Why do you think some people in the marketing department think that _____?" "What are you going to do if your decision is rejected entirely?" "You might not be aware of _____." "Don't you think everyone in this department recognizes the problem and wants it solved?" "They just don't want to decide it for themselves." "They want you to be the decider." "It wouldn't be the end of the world if _____ happened, would it?"

Timing of the Decision

Another variable that can play an important part in decision making is the timing that is operating in the target decider's mind as he/she deliberates with themselves or others, like an advisory committee. In their book, *Selling Yourself to Others: The New Psychology of SALES,* Hogan and Horton note that if you can change a person's frame of reference in regard to time, it will help them make wise decisions.[5] Any insurance salesman wants to talk about their product in terms of the future. They want to warn the target that inflation will take away some of the policy's value when it is cashiered. If they talk in terms of the present, their target thinks about the product in terms of the present-day purchasing power of the annual premium to be paid—it's sort of steep. Isn't it? If they think about the product in terms of the past, they will over value the size of the policy, giving it the purchase power of twenty years ago, and will decide not to buy the appropriate size of policy for their needs. Suppose further that this person is also known to be very close-minded and always certain that they are 100 percent right all the time. Let's also say that this person states a fact about the topic or issue (e.g., insurance is not a good retirement strategy) that you know or suspect is quite the opposite. If you say something contrary to that like "Well, I know for a fact that recent studies show that to be fallacious," you are going to get into a huge argument that you'll certainly lose.

Give the person a means of saving face, and saving face will offer you, the influential persuader, the opportunity to present the contradictory data that may result in making a different decision. A similar tactic discussed earlier is to admit the possibility that you are wrong or that your case is weak. Begin by saying something like this script: "Well, I could be wrong here. I am frequently, but in some cases I ran up against recently, it surprised me to discover that _____, and as a result, they avoided a costly error." Again, the underlined words are gentle escape doors for the closed mind.

Good rules for influential persuaders is to keep escape options open for your prospect or audience when they are moving to a decision. Keep asking them questions about the decision so they can move through the various steps or branches of the Decision Tree.

Let's now look at what motivates people to buy, join, donate, recruit, and other decisions because motives are probably what lie beneath the decision to decide in the first place.

TAKEAWAYS

After reading this chapter, you should be able to:

1. Help clients to use the Decision Tree to Take Ownership of their decisions.
2. Use the Decision Tree to help prospects Focus on their decision options.
3. Use the Decision Tree to help prospects to Narrow their decision options.
4. Use the Decision Tree to help prospects to Concentrate on their decision options.
5. Use the Decision Tree to help prospects to Finalize their decision options.
6. Apply the Decision Tree model to identify your prospect's or audience's default position(s).
7. Reinforce your prospect's and/or audience's final decision.
8. Give your prospect and/or audiences ways to save face should their decision not work out.
9. Help your prospect(s) and/or audience(s) Frame their decision in terms of its risks, opportunities, and timing.

10

THE MOTIVATIONS
FOR TAKING ACTION

This chapter focuses on what motivates people to buy, vote, join, donate, commit, affiliate, compete, convert, try, take certain actions, and other types of human behavior. In addition to the common motivators of punishment and reward, we will explore less frequently thought of motivators like self-satisfaction, the building of goodwill, the building of one's credibility, the accumulation of goods or mementoes, improved charisma or image, conviction related to good reasoning and evidence, and several others rooted in proven social scientific research patterns.

MOTIVATION: A TRAGIC EXAMPLE

On October 2, 2017, a 64-year-old retired man in Las Vegas opened fire with several automatic weapons on a large crowd listening to an open-air concert. He killed at least fifty-nine persons and wounded in excess of five hundred others. It was the largest number of persons killed and wounded by a single gunman in U.S. history. Naturally, governmental and law enforcement authorities, journalists, the relatives of the killed and wounded, and the general public want to know what could possibly motivate an apparently peaceful and law-abiding senior citizen to open fire at such a crowd. After all, he only had one traffic ticket in his entire life and had a net worth of $2 million. His relatives and neighbors described him as apparently harmless. They had no idea of the size, quantity, and variety of the weapons stashed in his apartment. He not only had regular and automatic rifles but also several handguns and large amounts of ammunition for both the rifles and the pistols, and he also had materials for making pipe bombs. He had a total of sixty-two weapons in addition to the one used to kill almost five dozen people in one incident alone. And you should know he had plans to visit other cities holding large, open-air concerts where he probably would have committed similar tragic killings.

Luckily, average influential persuaders do not need to know of his motivations, but they do need to learn about the various motivations of regular, normal, and non-lethal prospect(s) and of general audiences in regard to their decisions to take actions like purchasing, voting, joining, donating, committing, soliciting, preaching, or any of a number of other actions. This chapter explains and gives both examples and "scripts" of various lengths for you to use as models for your attempts.

SCRIPTS THAT TAP INTO MOTIVATION

This chapter attempts to discuss and provide sample "scripts" for tapping into such normal motivations when trying to influence and persuade. The scripts are only examples because like earlier ones they are meant to be altered and adapted by you to fit your own unique situations, persuasive aims, and prospect(s) or audience(s). These motives range from simple, almost common-sense ones, to other much more complex ones. But many motives are also as powerful as scientifically proven ones. These require not only learning but also testing on various audiences and in various circumstances and ultimately adopting or rejecting some.

This depends on your needs and the persuasive situation and its limitations. For instance, one such motivation which most people use in training their pets (and in some cases their children) is the motivation to avoid punishment. While it has proven far inferior to another motivator—giving rewards—it is not always available to the influential persuader trying to sell, recruit, solicit, convert, or motivate many other common actions. Many actions occur almost nonconsciously, such as opening the door for a person on crutches. In some cases, such actions are taken even when doing so endangers oneself. That was the case in Las Vegas when persons running away from the shooting stopped to help one of the persons wounded. Apparently, the unconscious mind simply takes action without regard to possible consequences. It just reacts. We are not going to spend much time on these motives. Rather, we are going to look at what motivates normal persons in normal situations to make purchases, cast votes, donate money, take oaths, and to take other actions.

FEAR AS A MOTIVATION

Fear is a normal motivation. Maybe we are afraid that if we are not on time to work, we'll lose our job; or we're afraid to be late for the test; or we'll disappoint our prospect; so, we set our alarm to wake us early enough to make the appointment. We also remember what it was like that morning when we forgot to set the alarm. That was nerve-jangling and very stressful. Fear and the resulting anxiety and stress have been studied in many experiments and have been very effective, especially when combined with highly effective and influential persuasion. But as mentioned earlier, sometimes it boomerangs or creates almost opposite unintended effects than those desired. For example, the fear of getting overweight is used in advertisements for costly diet programs, and sometimes it causes the target to go on secret eating binges, often with chocolate. Maybe we are afraid that we'll be all alone when we take a bad fall, so we are great prospects for the "Life Alarm" device that is better than calling 911.

Most of us fear growing old, so we join health clubs to keep young and in shape, and we try to keep up with the fashions of the day and interact with others in groups of all ages. We may become volunteers for some worthy cause or organization to keep ourselves active. And there are a host of other things including maintaining our health through regular check-ups with a family doctor. Or we fear what others will think of our self-image if we are out of fashion, so we spend lots of money on clothes, cosmetics, hair styling, or taking up a new sport or interest like curling or yoga.

We buy self-help books or go to unnecessary short courses to improve our self-image. Maybe we fear being poor, especially if we were poverty stricken in our youth. As a result, we become fixated with being extremely thrifty, and so we avoid spending money on frills, or we become an investor in gold, or we might even become a hoarder accumulating needless stuff because we worry about the greedy motives of others.

Some people fear that other people might cheat them. Why are they so nice to us? They might want to fool us, so we don't do business with them. As a result, we lose opportunities to learn from them and to enjoy their company, and the fear of losing continues to haunt us. Many become paranoid about the motives of others, and the motivation of fear simply multiplies exponentially.

EMOTIONS AS MOTIVATION

Management and communication consultant Dr. Kevin Hogan is convinced that most purchase behavior is motivated by emotions like fear, hate, sorrow, anger, joy, greed, and many others. He believes that people generally do not make purchase decisions for rational or logical reasons, but instead we buy products and brands of various things because of our emotional feelings about those things.[1]

PROBLEM/SOLUTION FORMAT AS MOTIVATION

One thing you can do for your prospects and/or audience(s) is to present the brand, candidate, good cause, or organization in a problem-solution format. Present your prospects/audience with a problem that is real and important to them. Remind them of the boring details and dreary headaches that accompany the problems of the day. After making them feel sorry for themselves, offer your brand, candidate, good cause, or organization as the ideal solution to that @#$%#$ problem. Provide your prospects and/or audiences with real, valuable solutions to their problems instead of false hopes. Tell them what things might be like in the future if they don't follow your advice.

Be certain that you present the problem right away and as if they were confronting it right there and right now. Let them stew in that for a while. Then tell them that you think you have a genuine, down-to-earth solution to their vexing problem. Don't lie to them. Present your advice or offer as a realistic solution—a clear alternative to the problems of the past and present, and then picture for them a problem-free future with no more of the aggravations of the past and the present. We all have problems for which we yearn for a reasonable and down-to-earth solution, and you can let your advice and/or offer be that yearned-for relief from their problematic challenges. Picture for them a future in which at least this annoying problem will no longer vex them.

OFFERS AS MOTIVATION

One of the questions I always ask of myself when facing a prospect's problem is what should be the nature of the *offer* I make to them. It's a critical query because what we want as consumers, managers, leaders, and representatives for others are two critical factors that are the yardsticks by which most reasonable people usually measure potential solutions. They are *Value* and *Quality*. Value is determined by cost. I had an interesting case of persuading and influencing a nursery manager who wanted and needed more traffic by potential customers to his nursery location. I suggested that the word "Free" was a proven one for attracting traffic. He thought that I was giving him the suggestion that his "Free" offer should be on shrubs or trees that might have had an actual cost to him in the hundreds of dollars.

After some questions back and forth, he realized that my actual suggestion was that his offer be a "free six-pack of annuals" that had a perceived value of $3 in the consumer's eyes because that is what they were usually priced at elsewhere. But the six-pack of annuals had an actual cost to him, the retailer, of only sixty cents. This offer not only brought customers to his place of business at a small cost, but they very frequently made other and often higher-priced items like tools, shrubs, work gloves, fertilizers, statuary, etc. Also, they will probably return to his business in the future, thus creating what marketing experts refer to as "The Lifetime Value of a Customer," as noted earlier.

A critical factor in moving merchandise works largely because of the power of the word "Free," which you'll remember has kept Cracker Jack going since the 1880s along with the idea of what was free was a *prize* and not a gift. That word seems to say that you have to do something special to win the prize. Of course, everyone knows that all you have to do to get the prize is simply to open the pack and find it. You see, words really do matter, as the difference between "prize" and "gift" demonstrates.

Sample Offers

A frequent offer in retail markets is known as the BOGOF which stands for "Buy One, Get One Free," which is very much like the offer of "Up to 50 Percent Off!" isn't it? The value here is quite good, so the consumer might be willing to look further into this offer. As mentioned above, the next thing that they would be likely to explore is the quality of the brand being offered at the two-for-one bargain. The brand of the type of product that a person is considering purchasing is usually a good indication as to quality. If it's a brand like L.L.Bean, you know the level of quality is going to be high, so you probably will make a purchase because of the very good value of getting two of the same brand for the price of one (BOGOF).

So, the combination of value and quality really can motivate you to make the purchase. When trying to convert prospects into clients, you should always try to make offers that are composed of high value and high quality. If the brand is unfamiliar to you, search online for its ratings or go to the Better Business Bureau website and type the word "ratings" and the brand name in the search box. This should give you enough information to know whether you are really offering good quality to go with the value dimension of the offer.

URGENCY AS A MOTIVATION

Another powerful motivator for most prospects and/or audiences is the idea of *Urgency*, or the feeling that one must move quickly and "Act Now!" or the offer will no longer be available. This emotional feeling of Urgency can be caused by several factors, and the motivation can be stirred by certain sets of words, as are usually indicated in the headline of the offer, so choose your headlines carefully. For instance, one cause of Urgency is a lack of time in which to act. That's the idea of limited sales hours, as in "These prices good for six more hours!!" or by the consumer's view on the television screen of a countdown-type timer that is supposed to show how many minutes remain while the offer is available at this price.

A third way to communicate the sense of Urgency and to convince the consumer audience to take action and place an order to buy the brand is to make a "But wait . . ." offer. This is used with television advertisements made by many brands that offer an extra set of the brand if the consumer telephones the number on the screen and orders right now. The words are printed on the television screen, and the announcer says something like "But Wait!! Order Now and We'll Send a Second Set Absolutely Free—And We'll Pay Shipping and Handling!"

SCARCITY AS A MOTIVATION

In addition to motivating prospects and/or consumers via the creation of a sense of urgency, another motivation jump-starter is to create the idea of *Scarcity* or that "Only a Few are Left!" The consumer had better get them before they are all gone, as "Not Many Are Left for This Season!!" When something is *perceived* to be in short supply, its *perceived* value necessarily goes up. It doesn't really matter what its real value is. What matters is what people believe it is worth. That's what really counts.

THE "TAKEAWAY" AS MOTIVATION

A famous sales technique known as "The Takeaway" utilizes the Scarcity principle very powerfully. The salesman offers great quality at a good value price to prospects or audiences and then takes the offer away, but guess what? It's the consumer's good luck that the offer has been reinstated, but only if they "Act Now!!" and the previously disappointed customer buys it up without much research or consideration. "There Are Only a Limited Number Remaining!" is another sample headline for "The Takeaway," and it uses the sense of urgency as well. It suggests that the offer is about to be taken away unless the consumer acts "Right Away!," and the phrase "I'm only in your area today and won't be able to take your order tomorrow!" also works. In matters of the heart, the "Hard to Get" member of the opposite sex is usually the most popular member of that sex. When successfully wooed and won, the "Hard to Get" person seems suddenly not all that great.

Other sample headlines can also trigger the Scarcity principle. The principle is particularly powerful when competition is perceived to be in play. That's what accounts for the huge crowds of shoppers in the marketplace on "Black Friday," as it is known. It's the day after Thanksgiving. Headlines that urge consumers to get out to the stores on their usual vacation day say things like "Don't Miss Out on Our Before-Christmas Clearance Deals!!" The headline is designed to *motivate* prospects and/or audiences to "Get There Early!" before all the marked-down merchandise is sold.

Even world politics is not immune. In the mid-1990s, Russians suddenly found more merchandise of all types on previously empty shelves due to Mikhail Gorbachev's *glasnost* policies. And they found that they had more freedom than ever before. A group of military and KGB leaders staged a countercoup and deposed Gorbachev. What once had been scarce became available and then was threatened with becoming scarce once again, so the populace staged riots and captured tanks that the military had ordered out to quell the protests. It took three days of nationwide protests—some violent—for the military and KGB plotters to admit defeat.

Robert Cialdini in his best-selling book, *Influence: The Psychology of Persuasion*, gives an interesting use of the competitive influence of the Scarcity principle. His brother Richard engaged in the old adage, "Buy Low; Sell High," on selling used cars. He bought good used cars low, shined them up, and advertised them, giving a phone number and then (and most importantly) scheduled interested prospects to show up and view the car on the same day and only minutes apart. Buyer number one arrived right on time and started the usual bargaining procedure, pointing out minor flaws and quoting lower-priced examples of the same vehicle in the local newspaper. Then buyer number two arrived, and then was perceived as real competition for the vehicle. While they squabbled, buyers number three and four arrived, thus increasing the competition. Richard made good use of the competition element in the Scarcity principle utilizing this technique.[2]

TIME AS A MOTIVATION

Time is also a commodity that can become scarce, as we all know when we are especially rushed and/or need to meet a deadline. Even lawyers realize its value by copiously keeping track of their "billable hours" as opposed to what you'd think was most important to the firm or the number of cases won and the financial size of the judgments/fines. But it's also important to most lawyers in medium-to-large firms to keep just as copious track of their non-revenue producing hours, or what are called their *pro bono* hours (i.e., those given to worthy causes for PR purposes) or the revenue produced by cases settled out of court.

Large firms expect their associates to log at a minimum of 2,000 such billable hours per year. That's forty hours per week times fifty weeks. In actuality they will have to work far more than forty hours per week, especially if they work pro bono hours as well. That makes billable hours the true commodity for which one gets financially rewarded. So, the same Scarcity principle applies there too. In other words, they are in competition for clients with lots of billable hours needed per year. So, there are a wide variety of motivations for taking action, many of which will be of interest to your prospects and/or audiences. I have researched, written, consulted, and taught about these other motivations elsewhere, and I'll summarize them briefly in the next few pages. If you are interested in reading about them further, I'd recommend that you read chapter 7 in my book which is titled *Persuasion: Reception and Responsibility*, and use the 13th edition. It's been used in colleges and universities across the country and in other countries as well since 1973 when the first edition was published.[3] In my book, I discuss human motivations and label them as "Process Premises" because I believe they are psychological processes that occur in our minds as we are receiving persuasive and influential appeals.

The first among these "Process Premises" are our biological needs and wants. You'll recall the differences between needs and wants from the sample scripted interaction with a good friend, the hypothetical prospect dentist Dr. Swenson, back in chapter 2. These needs and wants include our need for *Emotional Security*, or the sense that the world is predictable in the ways we suppose that it is thought to be or as it used to be.

That's why events like the attack of 9/11/01 was so disturbing to everyone. Thousands of persons working in a huge and modern pair of high-rise office buildings lost their lives as these large buildings collapsed and buried them as a result of having two jet airliners purposely crash into them, causing such extreme heat that the buildings' infrastructure could no longer support the weight of them. That kind of event can certainly cause emotional distress for all who witnessed it in reality or over their television sets. People wondered if the United States was under a surprise attack similar to the Japanese naval and air attack on Pearl Harbor, Hawaii, that happened on December 7, 1941, and which led to the U.S. entry into World War II.

Our need for Emotional Security was threatened on 9/11/01, and so the entire country was motivated to take actions to try to restore it. All commercial air traffic was suspended, and when the Pentagon was also attacked by a commercial airliner, killing many more, the country went on a wartime basis. The president was whisked away from an event that had him reading a story to a group of primary schoolchildren, and he was taken to a national security location. Our need for Emotional Security had been threatened, and we were willing to take drastic actions like the establishment of a department of "Homeland Security" and declaring a war against terrorism. Another of our human needs is to be appreciated for our value to others and their appreciation for our contributions. You'll recall my earlier description of how workers compared with managers in the ranking of factors in job satisfaction. The workers rated "Appreciation for work done" as the number-one factor in job satisfaction and "My boss listens to me" in position number two. Those results certainly provide evidence of one's self-worth. As our society becomes more globally oriented and human interactions occur—sometimes mainly via social media networks (SMNs) like Facebook—our need to be reassured of our individual worth will surely increase.

Not only are we motivated by our needs and wants for appreciation as members of the greater society, but we are also motivated by getting feedback that we are above average in some way or another. This positive emotion motivates us to seek it out from family, neighbors, co-workers, and groups like our church, local civic organizations such as the Rotary or Kiwanis clubs, and even groups like a local softball team.

THE NEED FOR ROOTS AS MOTIVATION

In a very mobile society such as ours where families move from one home to another and frequently in a different zip code, city, or state, people seem to want to have a feeling of being "from __X__ somewhere," and when introducing themselves to another person will say something like "Well, I'm originally from _____." Or "Well, my roots are in . . . state." And most people tend to remain rooted to that place for much if not all of their lives. It's why there are family or high school reunions. They give us a feeling of having roots which is at the very least a want if not a need.

MASLOW'S PYRAMID OF NEEDS AS SIGNS OF MOTIVATION

Well-renowned psychologist Abraham Maslow[4] maintained that our needs were hierarchical and that there were five needs and/or wants in everyone's psyche. The most essential and therefore basic needs were those needed for survival, such as food, water, air, sex, etc. He labeled them as our *Basic Needs*—they were not just a "wants" but essential needs. Until they were satisfied, other needs, and /or wants were unlikely to emerge.

Above them in his pyramid or hierarchy were needs for what he called our *Security or Safety* needs, by which he meant not only safety from harm but also safety and security in our ability to keep meeting our basic needs.

Above this level of needs came a level of wants—perhaps the want—for others to belong to or with. These he labeled *Affiliation or Belonging* needs/wants, which means a sense of identification with others. They might be needs that could be met by one's family, an organization like a service club such as Kiwanis or Rotary, the company one works for, a political party, and other organizations.

Above these in Maslow's hierarchy came what he called our *Esteem* wants. He thought we wanted to be held in high favor with the others with whom we felt this sense of identification. This could include being chosen as a leader, receiving prestige awards, or getting simple thanks for the work we have done for the group with which we identify,

At the top of his hierarchy came a category of *Wants* which Maslow labeled *Self-Actualization*, or the ability to live up to our own potential as measured by the self and others. Later in his life he associated this level of hierarchy with what he called *Peak Experiences*. These could be innovative concepts of treating some disease or of the workings of some machine or organization. I'm not exactly sure what he meant by this term, but I certainly would label the births and relationships with my two daughters as peak experiences in my life, especially when considered together with the more than fifty years of my marriage to my wife.

Another of these process premises is the whole range of our emotions, some of which we discussed earlier, like Fear/Anger and Pleasure/Pain. In addition to those emotions are feelings of *Guilt*, which is usually associated with feelings of *Shame*, and not just in the "You should be ashamed of yourself" or in the "Shame on you!" sort of berating of oneself or others but something much more motivating. It's almost as if one has to do something to purge oneself of the guilt and shame.

Of course, on the opposite side of the Shame coin comes the emotional feelings of self-pride. Or it might be the expression by others of how they are proud of you. As a child and later as a parent, I think I never felt better than when someone—my spouse, a parent, my children, a teacher, a boss, a member of an organization that is important to me, etc.—said that they were proud of me, and I try to tell my children how very proud I am of them as often as I can.

There's another pair of emotions that should be motivating to everyone, and they are *Happiness and/or Joy*, and not in the "Happy Birthday" sense but instead in the highly motivational feelings one gets when everything seems to be going according to plan. It's as if you are succeeding in meeting and satisfactorily fulfilling what life's syllabus has in store for you. Other emotions include feelings of relief, hope, compassion, sympathy, and many others.

A third kind of process premise that can be highly motivating for some are the *Attitudes* which each of us has that relate to actions we or others take, experiences that we have, people whom we meet, objects which we own or wish to own, political issues, and more. They are a tendency or an intention to behave in certain ways. They could be in reference to something as simple as a kind of vegetable such as broccoli or something as serious as our political beliefs or our ideology of life.

We are motivated to verbally express them out loud sometimes, but we want to let others know who we are and in what we believe. You'll often meet measurements of your attitudes in those rating sheets that range from one to ten and you are asked to rate something as "Highly Favorable" at the top ten of the scale and "Highly Unfavorable" at the other end of the scale. Closely related to one's attitudes and also very motivating are one's beliefs and opinions. They also qualify as process premises. In terms of which might be most difficult and most easy to change using persuasion and influence, I'd put opinions at the easy end of the continuum and beliefs at the difficult-to-change end of the continuum, with attitudes in the middle. Nonetheless, each can be a motivator to many persons whom you want to persuade and influence.

A fourth and more difficult to explain kind of process premise can be both a need and a want and in several ways. This is the need/want to experience *Consistency* between and among actions, events, people, places, attitudes, beliefs, opinions, and so on. You'll notice that this process meshes with others we've already discussed. Whatever the case, most people like to live in and experience a predictable world. You'll remember that *consistency* is among the words that we associated with one's credibility. Our need/want for consistency was violated in the terrorist attacks on the twin towers of New York and the Pentagon on 9/11/01, which motivated the entire nation to do things differently and resulted in massive social changes that are with us to the present day. When the world behaves in accord with our predictions for it, we feel and are highly motivated when this consistency exists, and the obverse is also highly motivating—we feel highly motivated when we meet or expect inconsistency in the way things, people, places, beliefs, etc. seem to be. The nursery manager discussed earlier felt inconsistent about my advice to offer something for free in order to induce consumer traffic at his place of business. The reason he initially felt very low motivation to follow my advice was he thought I meant expensive items in his inventory. He felt perfectly consistent when I explained that I meant he should make a "Free!" offer of a high profit/ low cost and inexpensive element in his inventory.

So, as you try to persuade and influence your prospects and/or audiences, try to give advice or make offers that are very consistent with the prospect(s) and/or audience(s) frame of mind, their beliefs, attitudes, and values or your own perception of their Objectives, Strategies, and Tactics referred to and exemplified way back in chapter 1.

TAKEAWAYS

After reading this chapter, you should be able to:

1. Identify several specific motivations that move normal people to take action.

2. Explain several sources of Fear as a motivation to buy, vote, join, volunteer, and many other kinds of action.

3. Describe and explain how and why the problem-solution format can motivate others to take any of the actions cited in Takeaway # 2 above.

4. Explain and give examples of "The Lifetime Value of a Customer," and you should also be able to use this concept to motivate your business prospects and/or clients that you hope to persuade to develop this value from their clients.

5. Explain and help your clients to use a Sense of Urgency to motivate, persuade, and influence others.

6. Explain and give examples of the BOGOF offer. What strategy is used with an offer?

7. Explain and give examples of the "But Wait!" strategy in telemarketing offers.

8. Explain how the Scarcity Principle worked in the deposing of a Russian premier and how the same principle helped Robert Cialdini's brother sell used cars.

9. Explain how Time is a commodity in the legal professions and elsewhere and how it might be used to motivate, persuade, and influence others to take the recommended actions of purchasing, voting, volunteering, joining, and other specific actions.

10. Discuss and give examples of each of the levels of motivation in Abraham Maslow's Pyramid or Hierarchy of Needs.

11. Define what is meant by the term *Attitude*, and describe how attitudes are sometimes measured.

11

PRESENT YOUR MESSAGE IN A CAMPAIGN

In today's digital world, most audiences usually receive most persuasive messages repeatedly, and many times it is also via various media. They see, read, or hear about products, candidates, services, etc. on media, such as television and radio commercials, out-of-home billboards and signs, printed packaging, leaflets and brochures, printed ads in publications like magazines or newspapers. Of course, they also see, read, and hear about opportunities and products online, on social media, news, shopping, and other websites. On buttons or imprinted T-shirts, baseball caps, and the rest.

As you prepare your proposal or "brand story," you must consider the number of "exposures" to your message that you want your target prospect and/or audience(s) to encounter, and which media you want to use besides yourself, the timing of the messages, and many other campaign factors discussed here. Campaigns are not just a collection of influential persuasive messages delivered over time. So, what are they, and what do they accomplish? They are a well-planned and extended narrative about a brand, candidate, worthy cause, organization, etc. The campaign should have well-thought-out and specific *Objectives*, *Strategies*, and *Tactics* that tell the "story" of a politician, brand, worthy cause, organization, etc. They have several characteristics.[1] For instance, if successful they usually:

1. Create a "position" or niche in the prospect(s)' mind.
2. Are designed to develop over time.
3. Dramatize the idea, person, product, or ideology to create personal connection.
4. Use sophisticated communication to reach certain targets in the audience.
5. Are like watching a good movie or television series.
6. Connect with the prospect/audience in a variety of ways.
7. And more.

Noted language philosopher Kenneth Burke describes five elements that he considers essential in some way to a balanced and logical narrative. They are (with slight explanations):

1. *The Scene or Setting* in which action is to or might occur—a "fitting container for the action that will or may occur" (e.g., The royal court of Denmark in *Hamlet* mentioned earlier).
2. *Acts which are appropriate* to the Scene (i.e., they "fit" with the Scene—this is not the case in *Hamlet*, as a ghost of his father is wandering the royal castle and his mother has remarried the king's brother very shortly after the king's death. In fact, Hamlet is disturbed that they used the funeral feast leftovers for the wedding reception).
3. *Actors or Agents* who can take appropriate or inappropriate Acts/Actions within the Scene (i.e., Hamlet disavows his "engagement" to Ophelia as a feminine figure who reminds him of his "foul" mother. Ophelia then goes insane and commits suicide).
4. *An Agency or Mechanism* which justifies certain Acts/Actions because of a philosophy or belief (i.e., Hamlet's father as a ghost demands revenge for his murder and the "incestuous" marriage of Hamlet's mother).

5. A *Purpose* that justifies or gives a reason for certain Acts/ Actions taken by the Agents/Actors in the Scene (i.e., Hamlet knowingly/and "accidentally" kills his uncle, the king, and his mother to avenge his father's murder and marital betrayal, thus restoring "royal balance" in the kingdom of Denmark).

Now let's try to put these five elements in place to tell a "Brand Story" that centers on an influential Persuasive Campaign. For our purposes, we'll try to promote a fall event in a small town that grew from a few persons more than sixty years ago to be participated in by an estimated more than one hundred thousand individuals and groups today. It is the Sycamore Pumpkin Festival in the relatively small town of Sycamore, Illinois, where I live. Let's further suppose that the Pumpkin Committee wants to increase attendance at the event and has hired you/me/us as their official promoter(s). First, I'll give some background on the festival.

Wally Doe, a local bicycle dealer, initiated the event by displaying several fancy decorated Jack-o-Lanterns on his front lawn way back in 1956 when the town's population was about sixty-five hundred. The next year and for a few years thereafter, more and more townspeople (and especially children) brought their decorated pumpkins to join his display. Soon thereafter Mr. Doe had an entire yard full. He then convinced local officials to display decorated pumpkins on the courthouse lawn. With help of the local Lion's Club, they also instituted a "Children in Costume" parade. And the Sycamore Annual Pumpkin Festival was born. Today the population of Sycamore is about eighteen thousand, and a statue of Mr. Doe is the official festival logo riding his super-high front-wheel bicycle. The festival has many activities, including a house walk of historic homes, jogging races of five and ten kilometers, an arts and crafts fair, two carnivals with rides (one for kids and the other for teens and adults), a downtown crowded with dozens of local and outside food and other vendors, and of course the highlight of the event, a two-and-a-half-hour-long parade that is viewed by approximately one hundred thousand persons. It's supposedly the second longest parade in Illinois.

THE YALE/BINDER MODEL OF CAMPAIGN DEVELOPMENT

I have written about the five stages of the Yale/Binder model of campaigns and movements elsewhere.[2] This model has been applied to many campaigns of various types—product, political, organizational, worthy cause, etc.

The Identification Stage

That model indicates that the first stage in most campaigns or movements is the *Identification* Stage, or the creation of a position or recollection in audience members' minds such that they identify certain characteristics, information, slogans, colors, and/or details of the focus or theme of the campaign. Our first persuasive influential message (sent via television, newspapers, as well as radio and printed media like brochures, billboards, signs, etc.) could also become a public service announcement in newspapers and on television and radio stations in nearby towns and in the Chicagoland area. It will be something like the following:

> "Imagine a snug, small town with lots of historic homes, fall colors, scrumptious food offerings, and active and happy citizens who for over sixty years have joyfully celebrated autumn and All Saints' Eve—now the second most financially active holiday in the year, second only to Christmas. It is the ultimate in children's spoofery and fun. Imagine this town filled with tons of activities (mostly free); house decorations; haunted houses with ghosts, witches, and goblins; and over a thousand pumpkins on display at the courthouse and at many homes, and all lighted for nighttime viewing. There'll be thousands of decorated pumpkin Jack-o-Lanterns on the courthouse front

lawn, walking tours of antebellum homes, a downtown filled with scores of local and regional vendors of food stuffs and products, and topped off by a free two-and-one-half-hour parade of floats, marching bands, clown troupes, celebrities like Wally Doe—Mr. Pumpkin—and local groups, horseback riders, animal trainers, plus much more—all touting their activities, many of which can be seen on YouTube."[3]

This message (and shortened versions for ten-second radio and television spots, festival buttons, flags and/or signs, imprinted calendars, T-shirts, baseball caps, and more) tells the story of the festival and might be accompanied with visual images of Mr. Doe on his old-fashioned bicycle (the festival's logo), Jack-o-Lanterns, pictures of the official Pumpkin Fest button, and pictures of a Jack-o-Lantern superimposed on a huge sycamore leaf. As much as possible, the printed and visual images would emphasize the colors of orange and black and the music and lyrics of "Everybody Loves a Parade." Appropriate public parade footage and/or images of various sizes and lengths will be developed so that they can be tailored to fit various size print and electronic advertisements or public service announcements. Copies would be sent to various newspapers and television and radio stations in the greater Chicago area. These details should also be included in all print materials promoting the festival.

THE YALE/BINDER MODEL OF CAMPAIGNS

This story would fix an image of what the event is like and could be included in public service television and radio commercials, printed public service messages, or ads in newspapers in surrounding towns and cities including Chicago and its suburbs, billboards placed on well-traveled roadways, and other printed signs, leaflets, and hand-outs. Any and all of these would make clear that the *Identification* in stage one of the Yale/Binder Model has been reached.

The Legitimacy Stage

People know about the festival in much of the Chicagoland area. This stage in the model is followed by a stage they call *Legitimacy* that authenticates the candidate, product/brand, movement, organization, worthy cause, etc. The fact that the festival is still alive and growing after more than sixty years testifies to its Legitimacy. The next stage in the Yale/Binder Model of Campaigns and Movements is labeled *Participation*, which is intended to get either real physical or symbolic involvement in the now legitimate campaign or movement by participants and audiences as well. It might involve having a bumper sticker, yard sign, T-shirt, or button endorsing the festival or political/social movement campaigns.[4] These media would promote the candidate or movement, as was the case in 2018 with the *Enough Is Enough* movement to make gun laws stricter. It is a well-known fact that persons who participate in campaigns in real or symbolic ways are more likely to vote for the candidate, the bond issue, or to buy the brand or service being promoted and other campaign activities. This is a compelling stage in assembling a crowd on the days of the pumpkin festival. It is important to design as many participative activities as possible as noted above and to promote them just as vigorously as one promotes the event itself.

The Participation Stage

The kinds of participative activity that the town audience might adopt or join already exist for townspersons in the decorated pumpkin display on the courthouse lawn and decorating their own houses with well-lit and spooky scenes, displaying the official pumpkin flag in the weeks preceding the festival, and of course participating in Halloween by handing out treats to the Trick or Treaters who come to one's house on Halloween Eve. But there should be some way for out-of-towners to participate in the festival. Of course, they can participate by coming to the festival, looking at the parade, house displays, the antebellum house walk, the crafts fair carnivals, and by looking at all the decorated pumpkins and sampling the food offerings in the downtown vendors' area. But what can they do prior to the festival to engage in the event? One thing would be to request information in the form of the official festival leaflet and to purchase and wear an official festival button. Another would be to purchase a festival button or flag. These should be mentioned in all publicity for the festival—commercials, billboards/signs, television and radio public service announcements, and other announcements in local, suburban, and Chicago newspapers. Also, out-of-towners could participate in a house walk, at arts and craft fairs, and other subevents (e.g., the pie-eating contest). The end result of the *Participation* Stage of Campaigns and Movements should be a sense of community and of unity among all of the persons participating—townspeople as well as out-of-towners.

The Penetration Stage

The fourth stage of the Yale/Binder model of Campaigns and Movements is called the *Penetration* Stage, and it signals the point at which the campaign/movement can be considered to have succeeded. It's when the brand has achieved a significant market share, the candidate has won office, legislation has been passed, or donations have surpassed the campaign goal. In the case of the sixty-second Pumpkin Festival, it will be when a surprisingly larger number of out-of-towners than before attend and participate in some of the activities. Whenever the competition in any campaign copies your campaign, brand innovation, new theme, activities, etc. you can be certain that you have successfully influenced and persuaded the public and your competitors. As they say, "Imitation is the highest form of flattery and respect." Other indications of Penetration might be winning third place in a first-time political run for office, an increase in public opinion polls, awards, or prizes for excellence, significant increases in donations, larger-than-ever crowds for events, adoption of your innovations by opposing movements, etc. Now it's time to show your appreciation to all who helped you achieve your goal.

The Distribution Stage

That leads us to the final stage in the Yale/Binder Campaign/ Movement Model called the *Distribution* Stage, and it is one of the ways one can show appreciation for all the help the campaign has received over its course. A winner in a political campaign/ movement usually sponsors a "Victory" event with food, drinks, and entertainment, or the victor can try to pass the legislation that was promised in the campaign or to bring about the incentives promised to members of the movement. In some cases, patronage jobs can be awarded (a newly elected mayor, governor, or president of the United States awards numerous such jobs). Brands that exceed sales expectations can be given more shelf space to display the brand in what are called "slotting allowances." They can reward users of the brand with rebates, sweepstakes, or merchandise "prizes" for proofs of purchase. Sometimes distribution can be awarded to the larger players in the campaign or movement—the committee chairpersons, the key brand dealerships, the highest-achieving participants, the top salespersons, etc. In many brand campaigns, top salespersons can receive financial bonuses, free spectacular trips abroad, new vehicles, or other major prizes. Or they can be awarded prestigious promising positions in the company, movement, or the next campaign. As a result, they can realize that they are succeeding and progressing up the ladder. Sometimes positions are even invented by the campaign/movement to give such satisfying feelings.

THE HIERARCHY OF EFFECTS MODEL

The Yale/Binder model is a useful one, but there are other models of campaigns that we will consider briefly. One is called the *Hier-*

archy of Effects model[5] and offers a series of increasingly effective stages that create an escalating likelihood of adherence to or adoption of the brand, candidate, good cause, religion, etc. on the part of campaign audience(s).

The Awareness Stage

The first step in this model is *Awareness* or the first inklings the audience might get of the presence of a new brand, candidate, worthy cause, etc. The same stage is needed by political candidates. At the beginning of the campaign, most first-time candidates are unknown to the press and eligible voters and potential volunteers. For these candidates (and for unknown brands or causes as well), gaining name awareness is essential. They try to develop name awareness by advertising, and making guest appearances on local, regional, or national radio or TV talk shows, thus giving the overall audience a brief introduction to their candidacy. Or they could try running in primary elections and hopefully winning.

The Learning Stage

The next stage in the Hierarchy model is called the *Learning* step. In this stage, the campaigner tries to educate the audience about the brand, candidate, good cause, or movement. This is usually done by increasing and extending the activities used in the Awareness stage and by adding more detailed information about the positions on issues of the candidate, the benefits of the brand, or the efforts of the good cause and so on.

The Liking and Preference Stages

This step is followed by the *Liking* and *Preference* steps, which are usually accomplished by image-building strategies such as image ads telling the "story" of the brand, candidate, or good cause. This "story" would consist of not so much factual details but emotional ones which will sketch out the "personality" or character of the brand, candidate, or good cause.

The Induce Trial Stage

The final stage in the Hierarchy model is to *Induce Trial* by offering free samples of the brand, candidate, or good cause, and giving the audience the chance to participate in the campaign by trying the brand, volunteering to assist the candidate, donating money to the worthy cause, or giving word-of-mouth testimony to other potential customers, voters, or donors.

THE POSITIONING MODEL

A third model of campaigns and/or movements is called the *Positioning* model and is premised on the idea that there are certain psychological memory "positions" or *niches* in the human brain that are usually occupied by a single or at most a limited number of brands, candidates, or causes.[6] If a campaign can get its brand, candidate, or good cause into one of these "positions," the ability to "recall" or remember it is greatly enhanced and frequently leads to adoption, votes, or donations. This leads to "Top of Mind Awareness" (TOMA), which is defined by occupying one of the top seven plus or minus two brands, candidates, good causes, etc. in the audience's minds.

Being First Position

Some examples of *Being First* in recent times are Lunchables, Blockbuster videotape and DVD rentals, and spray chalk. Now what brand was the first chewing gum company's offering? It was Wrigley's Spearmint, of course. Who invented the first automobile or "horseless carriage"? If you said "Henry Ford," you are wrong!

Ford invented the assembly line; Mr. Nicola Benz invented the first automobile, and it was in Germany. The Duryea brothers invented the first American auto. So, you see the value of occupying the position of *Being First* in the Top of Mind Awareness in the consumer's mind. What are some of the other "positions" in the Trout and Reis Positioning model?

Being the Best Position

Being the Best is another position/category depicted in the model. In the frozen turkey category, Butterball occupies "The Best" niche in most markets. Consumers usually use the yardsticks of quality and value in making such determinations about positions in most categories. In the imported auto category, Mercedes-Benz, Jaguar, and BMW are candidates for *Being the Best*, but there are others. *Being the Best* in the "Worthy Cause" category (rated on financial performance, transparency, and accountability) are the Rotary Foundation, Direct Relief, and Map International—they tie for first according to Charity Navigator.

Being the Least Expensive Position

Being the Least Expensive is another "position"/category and is occupied by such brands as Dollar General, Walmart's "Everyday Low Prices," and Menard's "Where You Always Save More Money!" *Being Most Expensive* is a similar position/category, and Rolex watches, Mont Blanc pens, and Chanel perfumes are examples of this position category.

Tell Me What You Are Not

Tell Me What You Are Not is a rather unusual position/category and frequently uses the prefix "Un . . ." to tell the consumer, voter, donor, or joiner why they are different from all the other brands, candidates, good causes, etc. 7-Up soft drink once advertised itself as the "Uncola" and went from being nearly bankrupt to being second in soft drink preferences.

The By-Gender Position

This is another strategy used by campaigns/movements, with such candidates as *Gentleman's Quarterly,* Virginia and Eve cigarettes, Victoria's Secret, Dr. O's 2018 ED Pill, Nike Women, Adidas, *Outdoor Life, Sports Afield, Sports Illustrated,* and *Field and Stream,* all of which are being positioned by gender.

Positioning by Age

Another powerful market position/category growing as the population ages is *Positioning by Age* and it includes all sorts of prescription drugs for various age-related maladies, the AARP organization, various health and life insurance companies, bathing tubs, "sleeper" beds, "stair climbing devices," and retirement programs.

THE DIFFUSION OF INNOVATION MODEL

Another theory or model about persuasive campaigns is the *Diffusion of Innovation* model, which came about through social scientific study of farm innovations with the spread (diffusion) of such "innovations" as crop rotation, contour ploughing, hybridization of corn and other seeds, confinement raising of chickens and hogs, and many others. The theory can be applied to any innovation such as robots, artificial intelligence, social media networks (SMNs), virtual reality, texting, driverless autos, or pilotless aircraft. Its founder, Everett Rogers, in his pioneering book, *The Diffusion of Innovation,*[7] cites four stages or steps through which innovations finally become an everyday reality in any given field.

The Information/Knowledge Stage

The first stage, called the *Information/Knowledge* stage, is when a potential adopter of the innovation gathers information and deeper knowledge of the innovation and what its benefits are claimed to be (e.g., the first adopters of Skype technology, promoting video images in email).

The Persuasion Stage

This knowledge then enters the second stage of the model or the *Persuasion* stage, in which the original adopter(s) begin to tell others about its benefits, costs, complexity or simplicity, and cites testimonials (see chapter 5) from well-known, highly successful adopters as well as ordinary users.

The Decision Stage

This leads to the third stage in the model or the *Decision* stage, where potential adopters decide to try and/or test the innovation on their own, sometimes under strictly controlled, experimental conditions.

The Implementation Stage

If the innovation proves out and provides the promised benefits at an acceptable cost, they adopt the innovation, and the process enters a fourth stage, or the *Implementation* stage, and the innovation is adopted by large numbers of adopters—company wide, industry wide, state wide, nation wide, or even globally.

The Confirmation Stage

The model then enters a fifth stage called the *Confirmation* stage where the adopter finalizes their decision and continues using it as a standard practice. The diffusion process is especially important in low education, highly diverse, third-world populations where seeing the benefits accrued by one's neighbors are the most powerful influence on inducing trial and leading to final persuasion and decision and confirmation to adopt the innovative practice on a wide scale. It soon is the common practice country wide.

THE SYMBOLIC CONVERSION MODEL

Finally, you might want to consider a theory of campaign/movement influential communication in what is known as *Symbolic Convergence Theory*, whose very name suggests the melding of various communication "bits" into a single kind of shared meaning. It was discovered by researchers of the kinds of communication occurring in task-oriented small groups—a familiar communication forum in many campaigns/movements and occurring in branding, politics, doing good works, on the job, and in various organizations.

Researcher R. F. Bales[8] observed a kind of communication in small, task-oriented groups which he called "Dramatizes" or "Dramatizing," and found that it sparked very lively and animated discussion by group members who frequently added to a real or hypothetical "Drama" initially brought up by one group member. The other members of the group sat up more erectly, gestured, and interrupted more. Later tests showed that during dramatization, there was increased body temperature and perspiration in group members, and especially as they added their own details to the by now group-produced drama. Bales labeled this activity "chaining out" and called its end product a "fantasy theme," suggesting that it resembled but was not quite reality. It was a shared but imaginative reality composed of both real and imagined communications and other elements joined by the convergence of separate fantastic but "real" contributions of meaning. Let's suppose that a group is trying to decide which kind of remote control should accompany their company's brand of television. They are considering matters like its color, size, if it should be voice or button controlled, and similar details:

Member B says, "I think the remote control should be black instead of white—it just seems . . . more . . . more, more—I don't know."

Member A adds, "Heavy, I'd say—Black is a heavy color, I think, or feel . . . sort of . . ."

Member C adds, "Well, that's the color of the boxes that most jewelry comes in."

Member A nods in agreement.

Member D says, "Just so it works real well—that's what I'd insist upon, don't cha think?"

The group nods agreement.

Member E observes, "Just so it's not too complex for the average guy to quickly figure out and is reliable too."

Member B states emphatically, "Yeah, not made from aluminum either!"

Member A adds, "And doesn't burn through too many batteries too fast!" nodding all the time. The group laughs at this.

Member C says, "What's wrong with aluminum? Beer cans are made of aluminum!"

The group laughs again.

Member B says, "Well, then, it should be black, heavy, reliable, not use a lot of battery power, and no aluminum please!!"

Everyone laughs and nods in agreement.

The group has "symbolically converged," and if you like, "invented" a remote control to accompany the video product that their company produces.

Bales calls most of the individual additions "fantasy links," but concrete additions like the color black, reliable, and low battery draw he calls "reality links." He would call the comment about aluminum a "fantasy link" in the chaining process.

In terms of what most genuine and influential persuasive campaigns focus on, the issues are more complex and sometimes even controversial, like, "What is North Korea up to with this nuclear warhead and rocketry business?" Or consider again the recent "Enough Is Enough" protests against the ease with which a very young person can acquire a military style AR-15 machine gun type firearm just about anywhere in the United States. The protest marches were conducted by very young high schoolers and teachers and other adult supporters and also included older youths and even parents and grandparents. The marches occurred on seven continents and in city after city across the United States, including Washington, DC, where an estimated eight hundred thousand marched, thus setting a U.S. record for protest crowd size.

If enough "fantasy themes" symbolically converge, Ernest Bormann, a follower of Bales, says they create a "Rhetorical Vision" by which the group and other groups create a symbolic reality that they share and are committed to enthusiastically.[9] This was certainly the case with the "#Enough Is Enough" protest, and it seems that continuing protest actions to control the spread and ease of obtaining firearms in the United States will continue and perhaps spread even further and wider. Idea campaigns and movements like this one usually involve extended discussions across months and even years and should aim to develop both fantasy and reality links. With exciting highly motivated issues, this happens almost automatically and frequently evolves their work into a Rhetorical Vision, as also happened for "China is poised to become the largest, most polluted, and most diverse trading economy on the face of the Earth!" Sometimes Rhetorical Visions can be triggered or defused with a single or even few happenings. An older but good example is the vision of global warming. It really took off with the release of the Academy Award-winning film by former vice president Al Gore, *An Inconvenient Truth.* The film set off a national controversy over the validity of the claims that there was a serious global crisis. Some argued that the noticeable warming trend was only a temporary thing and compared it to previous warming trends. On the other side were those who insisted the trend had a cause—the pollution caused by the release of hydro carbons into the atmosphere. These substances were the fault of automobile exhausts worldwide and the massive amounts of coal being burned to generate electricity and for other reasons. Later, persons objected to the words "global warming" as too vague, and believers switched to the words "climate change" or "climate warming" as more acceptable to the general public. Today the debate goes on despite international agreements to reduce the level of hydro carbons being released into the atmosphere. One such agreement was the Paris Accords to which the United Sates had agreed but from which it withdrew with the election of Donald Trump. The controversy continues to the present day. There have been thousands of studies using Symbolic Convergence Theory as a basis. Many highly propagandistic attempts at influential persuasion have tried to spark a Rhetorical Vision. Enter the words "People for the American Way," and you will see an example of such propagandistic attempts. There are several commonly used and recurring "templates" for sparking such fantasy themes and Rhetorical Visions, mainly using familiar sports metaphors such as the baseball game with fantasy themes around such old favorites as "the final innings," the "7th Inning Stretch," or "Stealing Home." Another is the horse race with themes about "Going into the Stretch," the "Odds-On Favorite," and "They're Out of the Gates" metaphors. Finally, the boxing match is another template with metaphors like "Still the Early Rounds," "Below the Belt," punches, and the "Knock-Out Blows" images. A fairly recent instance of this type of vision was the establishment of the jihadist group ISIS and the rhetorical vision of being societally threatened with early blows of the Rhetorical Vision of globally engineered and implemented terrorism. Though the movement was attacked vigorously, it still seems to exist.

Symbolic Convergence Theory has been used in less ideological ways; for example, to "write" the perfect political campaign speech; to pass state regulations to permit riverboat casinos in Iowa; to recruit physicians to small towns; to train firefighters; to write scripts for weekly television dramas; and to sell agricultural products to hog farmers, to cite a few of the more practical and less ideological applications of the Symbolic Convergence Theory of campaigns and/or movements.

When planning, evaluating, or considering the Persuasive Campaign, we shouldn't forget that it is composed of a series, not a single, influential persuasive message that begins with an *Objective*, which is then put into action by one or a series of *Strategies* that are operationalized by using various *Tactics* (e.g., see chapter 1 of this book), which are exemplified here by the typical or sample "scripts" which I have provided for you throughout and that you can adapt for your own particular persuasive challenges. We should also remember that all persuasion is to some degree "self-persuasion" in which prospects and/or audiences are searching for "good reasons" to believe, change, and act or behave in the ways suggested by the influential persuaders. Be sure to remember that as you prepare to persuade and influence them. Let us now move on to the final chapter, which focuses on "Calls to Action" that can help you convince others to listen to and perhaps reward you for your advice and/or offers as well as some ideas concerning how you might promote your skills, and some "Persuasion Ethics" plus a few more pieces of influential persuasive advice.

TAKEAWAYS

After reading this chapter, you should be able to:

1. Recognize that your objective of getting what you want is more probable the more times your prospect(s) and/or audi-

ence(s) are exposed to your persuasive and influential proposals. This is most efficiently done in a campaign that runs over time and uses several media. So, you need to be planning to run your proposals/offers in a campaign or models which are covered in this chapter.

2. Create a sense of *Identification* for your persuasive and influential services via a campaign. You'll need to create a name for your services. Perhaps something like "I Persuade/Influence Others" would work. Its acronym IPIO tells your prospect(s) very little. Be creative and brainstorm this with existing clients, friends, or ask for help from a professional name and logo firm.

3. Focus your campaign around a memorable event, festival, or idea that is not politically focused in any way. And give your service(s) a sense of *Legitimacy* by citing existing or former clients who have been pleased and satisfied with your work. Testimonials are powerful here, as is the mention of how long you have been providing those services (e.g., "Providing services for over ten years").

4. Get participation with your campaign by giving your prospect(s), existing clients, and/or other audiences a visible reminder of your service (e.g., a pen or magnet business card with your name and logo imprinted on it and urge them to recommend your services). You can offer them some kind of reward for doing so (e.g., a price reduction in your services to them).

5. Sponsor a *Distribution* event for existing clients (e.g., a picnic, bar-b-q, or community event ticket or tour).

6. *Induce Trial or Implementation* by prospect(s) and/or audience(s) by offering a money-back guarantee if they aren't satisfied with your services.

7. Consider using a ninety-minute focus group for five to seven persons to discuss your services. You could use existing or former satisfied clients and/or paid volunteer prospect(s) as participants by offering a free or reduced-price trial of your persuasive and influencing services on their behalf. The re-

sults of your listening to and analysis of the tape-recorded
group discussion might give you ideas for slogans, special
offers, etc. because of the dynamics of Symbolic Conver-
gence Theory. It's proven of value in a multitude of politi-
cal, sales, donation, volunteer recruitment, organizational,
joining, and other campaigns.

12

CALLS TO ACTION, THE ETHICS OF PERSUADING AND INFLUENCING OTHERS, AND PROMOTING ONE'S SKILLS

An obviously true statement in Robert B. Cialdini's best-seller, *Influence: The Psychology of Persuasion,* is the following quote: "People simply like to have reasons for what they do."[1] And I guess I'd add that they'd like the reasons to be *good reasons* versus poor reasons. You probably picked up this book partially due to its title that offers you eleven ways to get what you want. Another reason you started reading it was because of its subtitle that offers you the chance to discover ways to persuade and influence others in this twenty-first century. And perhaps you've realized that by now you have some of those skills, and as a result, you have a repertoire that can be extremely useful and marketed to businesses, candidates, organizations, worthy causes, and others. I hope to give some ideas about how to do that.

ETHICS AND ACTION STEPS

In the final analysis, every influential persuader wants prospect(s) and/or their audience(s) to effect or enact change in some verifiable way, and this usually means taking some specific *action* such as purchasing, voting, joining, donating, or changing beliefs or behaviors. As a result of becoming able to persuade and influence others, there are certain obvious ethical issues involved for you as you put the principles that you have learned here into action. Some of these ethical action steps are:

1. **Give** complete instructions for the desired action that you want your prospect(s) or audience(s) to take and in clear and specific terms to them. If possible, have them repeat it back in complete, clear, and specific terms as well so that you know that they understand.

2. **Remember** to ask if they have any questions and if they understand any details that must be followed. When working with a political candidate, it's not enough to ask the voter to go out on election day and vote for the candidate. Make sure that they are registered and know to vote at a certain location for their place of residence. Be sure to tell them that they must bring the appropriate form or forms of identification with them (e.g., driver's license or other form of photo identification). They need to know where their polling place is located, its hours and day of operation. Prospective voters must know and recall such details. Send reminders to potential customers when a promotion is ending. Call a colleague before a big presentation to make sure you're on the same page. Whatever your situation, help others to remember what their role is.

3. **Be specific** in the pricing of your services. You want your first-time prospects and/or audience(s) to become repeat customers or regular clients. Outline your political platform. Detail your action plan for building your new business headquarters. Whatever it is, be clear and specific.

4. **Refrain** from using manipulative or unethical persuasion tactics. (See my *Persuasion: Reception and Responsibility*[2] for a more detailed explanation.)
5. **Promote** your persuasive and influential skills and services in ethical ways.

You will undoubtedly notice that all five of these admonitions begin with an imperative or action-requesting verb—*give, remember, be, refrain,* and *promote*. The persuasive and influential advice you are going to give others should also use such action-giving or imperative verbs. Here are a few that give orders or instructions: *Try, Go, Buy, Get, Take, Visit, Drive, Hit, Obtain, Ask, Make, Put, Pass, Exercise, Give, Shall, Come, Eat, Have, Do Not, Should, Sing, Crawl, Run, Creep, Could, Steal, Use, Let, Write, Promise, Find, Must, Threaten, Entice, Choose, Seduce, Suggest, Invite, Close, Open, Look, Listen, Say, Touch,* and *Command* to name a few. You're very likely to find exactly what you need and want by using the thesaurus on your computer. Then combine that imperative verb with exactly what it is you want, as in "Ask *for directions*" or "Give *an answer*" or "Drive *to the bank drive-up window and be sure to get a receipt for the deposit.*" You can see the importance of being clear and precise when you want your prospect(s) to take specific action(s). You should also make sure that the final steps on your web page are a satisfying "landing strip" that congratulates the prospect for accomplishing the task and makes them feel pleased with themselves. Words like "Great" or "Way to Go!!" can energize prospects to take seriously the actions that you suggest.

There are a few other ethical things to call to your attention. It is generally considered *unethical* for a persuader to:

1. Accept some persuasive or influential fact or tactic simply because it is legal.
2. Accept the use of an unethical or dishonest means or tactic simply because it will help you to reach some desirable end result.

3. Intentionally falsify some statistic, quote, or fact. Some people maintain that there are things called *alternative facts*, but what they mean is that there is information that could lead to an opposite conclusion.
4. Stigmatize or victimize persons or groups that are your opponents on an issue.
5. Use information that denigrates what it means to be a human being.
6. Use what is clearly "hate speech."
7. Invent or falsify evidence.
8. Use faulty logic or reasoning.
9. Falsify positive testimonials about your skills at persuading and influencing others.
10. Reject or dismiss negative testimonials about your skills at persuading.
11. Use persuasion or influence that could undermine the First Amendment of the U.S. Constitution, which affirms freedom of speech, religion, assembly, petition, and freedom of the press to report its findings or editorial positions on issues.

So much for the "don'ts," but there are a few "dos" to keep in mind also.

1. Share your findings with your prospect(s) and audience(s) even if they are counter to your advice.
2. Double and triple check your findings and "facts" as carefully as you can.
3. Ask if there is a different way that your prospect(s) and/or audience(s) could get the same results as those you offer.

Remember that the digital age should carry with it the right to privacy, the ownership of intellectual property (like your advice and ideas), and freedom from digital deception techniques.

These ethical practices will assist you in persuading and influencing others while you maintain your credibility and self-respect as well as the respect of others. I hope that you keep them in mind as you persuade and influence others in the future. Now let's turn to the idea of marketing your skills to prospects and/or audiences.

IDEAS FOR MARKETING YOUR SKILLS IN PERSUASION AND INFLUENCE

I'm going to assume that your access to financial resources are limited but that your creativity is not. Remember that before the invention of books, magazines, newspapers, radio, television, etc. that there were *signs* outside or in or on one's place of business to call the public's notice or attention to the availability of goods and/or services (e.g., apples, grapes, meat, potatoes, pasta, advocacy, medical services, etc.). They were nothing fancy or very expensive, but sometimes they were very creative. That's what I'm going to advise for you here.

If you want to market your newly developed skills and service at persuading and influencing others, you'd probably want to do it in as inexpensive a way as possible. So, what might be some of these inexpensive ways or signs that could let others know that you have studied (and probably even practiced) being persuasive and/or influential? The least expensive physical sign that I can think of is the profile you can honestly create on inexpensive business cards that can be handed out when you call on potential prospects (e.g., businesses, service providers, churches, organizations, etc.). Then there is your profile on widely visited social media networks like Facebook, Twitter, LinkedIn, and others that may be specific to your needs. Spend some hours getting on and setting up those free profiles; some of these outlets also have services you can pay for to promote your business or your profile. Visit the profiles of members who seem to be likely prospects, and comment on their entries to let them know what your skills at persuasion and influence are. Invite them to join a group that you have already formed and see where that might lead. If this doesn't get you some prospects, spend some time creating an innovative profile for yourself and spend simply an hour a day responding to likely entries. Be sure to put your name and list your talents at persuading and influencing as interests or educational resources. The whole idea is to get yourself known for what you do.

Responses to the want-ads in the "Positions Wanted" or "Services" sections of the classified ads in the local newspaper can identify potential prospects and are relatively inexpensive. Your ads in the newspaper classifieds should stress your abilities at persuasion and influence. Craigslist has an entire section devoted to services. If you or anyone you know have graphic and design abilities, you could even develop an inexpensive brochure that can be left with potential prospects (e.g., art and marketing departments at a local college or university might want to have their students do such work, and again the paid internship is a possibility). There will be some expenses to have the brochure printed if you can afford that. Consult individuals and/or groups and organizations that provide similar services for businesses, churches, worthy causes, etc. and see if they will assist you in spreading the word about your service, product, or message.

In conclusion, I hope I've given you additional skills for being more influential and persuasive at work and in your community. Some of these strategies, when practiced regularly, may help you in your personal life as well.

TAKEAWAYS

After reading this chapter, you should be able to:

1. Ethically persuade and/or influence others to help you get what you want.
2. Understand the ethical don'ts and dos and practice them in your persuading and influencing of others.
3. Be able to motivate your prospect(s) to take action.
4. Be able to market your skills in inexpensive ways.

NOTES

2. MAKING A LASTING, CREDIBLE, PERSUASIVE, AND ETHICAL FIRST IMPRESSION

1. www.marksdailyapple.com/the-power-of-touch/.
2. www.careerbuilder.com/Article/CB-431-Getting-Hired-Six-Tips-for-a-Perfect-Handshake/.
3. www.en.wikipedia.org/wiki/Haptic_communication#Social.2Fpolite.
4. www.businessballs.com/body-language.htm#six-universal-facial-expressions.
5. www.sparkpeople.com/resource/wellness_articles.
6. www.businessballs.com/body-language.htm#six-universal-facial-expressions.
7. www.wofs.com/index.php/miscellaneous-mainmenu-38/567-body-language decoded.
8. www.forbes.com/sites/carolkinseygoman/2013/08/21/12-body-language-tips-for-career-success/.
9. http://www.entrepreneur.com/article/217491).

4. CREATE A RECIPROCAL RELATIONSHIP BETWEEN YOU AND YOUR PROSPECT(S)

1. Robert B. Cialdini, *Influence: The Psychology of Persuasion.* New York: HarperCollins Publishers, 2007.
2. www.searchquotes.com/quotes/author/Richard_Leakey/2/popular.
3. Cialdini, *Influence.*
4. Cialdini, *Influence*, 18.
5. Lionel Tiger and Robin Fox, *The Imperial Animal.* New York: Holt, Rinehart and Winston, 1971.
6. Cialdini, *Influence*
7. www.npr.org/blogs/health/2012/11/26give-and-take-how-the-rule-of-reciprocation-binds-us.
8. www.copyblogger.com/remarkable-content.
9. Kevin Hogan, *The Science of Influence: How to Get Anyone to Say YES in 8 Minutes or Less.* Hoboken, NJ: John Wiley and Sons Inc., 2011.

6. USE "SOCIAL PROOF" TO PERSUADE THE PROSPECT(S)

1. Robert B. Cialdini, *Influence: The Psychology of Persuasion.* New York: Harper Collins, 2007. (See especially chapter 4.)
2. Aileen Lee, *Social Proof Is the New Marketing.* See www. techcrunch.com/2011/11/27/social-proof-why-people-like-to-follow-the-crowd/. Tech Crunch. Accessed May 2, 2018.
3. Cialdini, *Influence.* 116.
4. Scott Detrow, *What Did Cambridge Analytica Do during the 2016 Election?* See www.npr.org/2018/03/20/595338116/what-did-cambridge-analytica-do-during-the-2016-election. National Public Radio/All Things Considered, March 20, 2018. Accessed May 2, 2018.
5. Lee, *Social Proof*
6. Ibid.
7. Ibid.
8. Cialdini, *Influence.*

7. KEEPING GROUP AND INTERPERSONAL DISCUSSIONS RELEVANT AND "ON TRACK"

1. Sarah Corbin Robert, *Robert's Rules of Order* (9th edition: newly revised). Glenview, IL: Scott Foresman, 1990.

8. BUILD YOUR OWN CREDIBILITY

1. www.huffingtonpost.com/alan-w-silberberg/artful-social-listening_b_1619218. Accessed May 12, 2018.
2. Kathryn Hatter, "How to Improve Active Listening Skills in Business Situations." chron.com. http://smallbusiness.chron.com/improve-active-listening-skills-business-situations-20192. Accessed May 12, 2018.
3. Kevin Hogan and James Speakman, *Covert Persuasion: Psychological Tactics and Tricks to Win the Game*. Hoboken, NJ: John Wiley & Sons Inc., 2006, 116–17.

9. MOVE TO A DECISION

1. Kevin Hogan, *The Science of Influence: How to Get Anyone to Say YES in Less Than 8 Seconds*. Hoboken, NJ: John Wiley and Sons Inc., 2011, 1–12.
2. Dale Carnegie, *How to Win Friends and Influence People*. New York: Simon & Schuster, 1936.
3. Robert B. Cialdini, *Pre-Suasion: A Revolutionary Way to Influence and Persuade*. London: Penguin Random House UK, 2016. (See especially pp. 11–18.)
4. Daniel Kahneman, *Thinking, Fast and Slow*. New York: Farrar, Straus, and Giroux, 2011. (See especially chapter 34.)
5. Kevin Hogan and William Horton, *Selling Yourself to Others: The New Psychology of SALES*. Gretna, LA: Pelican Publishing Inc., 2002.

10. THE MOTIVATIONS
FOR TAKING ACTION

1. Kevin Hogan, *The Science of Influence: How to Get Anyone to Say YES in 8 Minutes or Less.* Hoboken, NJ: John Wiley and Sons, Inc., 2011.

2. Robert B. Cialdini, *Influence: The Psychology of Persuasion.* New York: HarperCollins Publishers, 2007, 268.

3. Charles U. Larson, *Persuasion: Reception and Responsibility.* Boston, MA: Wadsworth and Cengage Learning; Canada: Nelson Education Ltd., 2013.

4. Abraham Maslow, *Motivation and Personality.* New York: Harper Collins, 1954.

11. PRESENT YOUR MESSAGE
IN A CAMPAIGN

1. L. Binder, *Crisis and Sequence in Political Development.* Princeton, NJ: Princeton University Press, 1971.

2. Charles U. Larson, *Persuasion: Reception and Responsibility,* 13th ed. Boston: Wadsworth/Cengage Learning Corp., 2013. (See especially chapter 11.)

3. Video footage of the parade can be seen at www.youtube.com/watch?v=8BRtnREmS-A.

4. Harry Rubenstein, *Campaign Button Will Survive Digital Age.* ZOCOLO Public Square (an Arizona State Knowledge Enterprise), November 7, 2016. See www.zocalopublicsquare.org/2016/11/07/campaign-buttons-will-survive-digital-age/chronicles/who-we-were.

5. R. J. Lavidge and G. A. Steiner, "A Model for Predictive Measurements in Advertising Effectiveness," *Journal of Marketing* 24, pp. 59–62. See also http://www.learnmarketing.net/hierarchy_of_effects_model.html.

6. J. Trout and A. Reis, *Positioning: The Battle or Your Mind.* New York: Harper & Row, 1986.

7. E. Rogers, *The Diffusion of Innovation.* New York: Free Press, 1962.

8. R. F. Bales, *Personality and Interpersonal Behavior.* New York: Holt, Rinehart & Winston, 1970.

9. Ernest G. Bormann, *The Force of Fantasy.* Carbondale: Southern Illinois University Press, 1985.

12. CALLS TO ACTION, THE ETHICS OF PERSUADING AND INFLUENCING OTHERS, AND PROMOTING ONE'S SKILLS

1. Robert B. Cialdini, *Influence: The Psychology of Persuasion.* New York: Harper Collins, 2007, 4.

2. Charles U. Larson, *Persuasion: Reception and Responsibility*, 13th Ed. Boston: Wadsworth, Cengage Learning, 2013, 313–20.

INDEX

accomplishments: cited for credibility, 85, 88–89, 97; political example past, 88
Achievers category, of business executives, 28, 30
action taking: audience motivation and, 125, 152; in Decision Tree model, 102, 109; marketing skills inexpensively, 152
actors or agents, as campaign element, 128
acts appropriate in scene, as campaign element, 128
agency or mechanism, as campaign element, 128
anecdotes, as persuasive evidence, 57
Aristotle, 44; communication channels, 44, 47–48, 49–50; Fear/Anger Appeal and, 47; on pleasure/pain principle, 49
arrangement, as persuasion stage, 44, 63
attributes, payoffs and, 13–14, 23
audience: campaigns exposure, 127, 144–145; motivation, for action, 125, 152; reciprocity, credibility and, 90, 91–92, 97; stories or narratives for audience attention,

40; in web pages, 40
audience analysis: of needs, 25, 29; qualitative research in, 25–26; quantitative research in, 25–26; of wants, 25, 29

bad choice fear, 22
Bales, R. F., 140
bandwagon effect example, of social proof, 66–67, 72–73
benefits, in demonstration, 62
Benefits versus Features approach, in persuasion, 52–53
be specific, as ethical action step, 148, 149
best position, in Positioning model of campaigns, 137
body language, 19, 153n4, 153n6
BOGOF. See Buy One, Get One Free
Bormann, Ernest, 142
Brand Story example, of campaign elements, 129–130
Brexit vote, in UK, 68–69
built-in obsolescence fear, 21
bulleted lists, in web pages, 38
business executives: Achievers category of, 28, 30; demographics on, 26–27; ethnographics on, 27,

ABOUT THE AUTHOR

Charles U. Larson, PhD, is the author of a best-selling textbook *Persuasion: Reception and Responsibility*, now in its 13th edition. He taught full-time at Northern Illinois University and is now emeritus professor. He served as "faculty intern" at J. Walter Thompson Inc. and with a small advertising agency in the Fox River valley area working with clients like "Lunchables," "Oscar Mayer Hot Dogs," "Clausen's Pickles," and "Vienna Beef Hot Dogs" and others. During his teaching career, he also worked as a consultant to and partner in several small but full-service advertising agencies until 2005. He has also written other books, book chapters, book reviews, and various publications in professional communication journals on topics such as political speeches, television advertising, persuasive campaigns, public relations, and salesmanship. Larson is often interviewed by radio and television news reports as well as newspapers. He still is the longest serving president of the faculty and staff assembly, executive secretary, and parliamentarian of the University Council at Northern Illinois University.